DATE DUE

GENES & DISEASE

DOWN SYNDROME

GENES & DISEASE

Alzheimer's Disease

Asthma

Cystic Fibrosis

Diabetes

Down Syndrome

Hemophilia

Huntington's Disease

Parkinson's Disease

Sickle Cell Disease

Tay-Sachs Disease

GENES & DISEASE

DOWN SYNDROME

F. Fay Evans-Martin, Ph.D.

CHELSEA HOUSE
PUBLISHERS
An imprint of Infobase Publishing

Down Syndrome

Chelsea House
An imprint of Infobase Publishing
132 West 31st Street
New York NY 10001

Library of Congress Cataloging-in-Publication Data

Evans-Martin, F. Fay.
    Down syndrome / F. Fay Evans-Martin.
        p. cm.—(Genes and disease)
    Includes bibliographical references and index.
    ISBN 978-0-7910-9644-4 (hardcover)
    1. Down syndrome. I. Title. II. Series.

    RJ506.D68E93 2008
    618.92'858842—dc22   2008044773

Chelsea House books are available at special discounts when purchased in bulk quantities for businesses, associations, institutions, or sales promotions. Please call our Special Sales Department in New York at (212) 967-8800 or (800) 322-8755.

You can find Chelsea House on the World Wide Web at
http://www.chelseahouse.com

Text design by Annie O'Donnell
Cover design by Ben Peterson

Printed in the United States of America

Bang NMSG 10 9 8 7 6 5 4 3 2 1

This book is printed on acid-free paper.

All links and Web addresses were checked and verified to be correct at the time of publication. Because of the dynamic nature of the Web, some addresses and links may have changed since publication and may no longer be valid.

CONTENTS

1

WHAT IS DOWN SYNDROME?

As a teenager, Chris Burke wanted to become an actor. His first acting role was in the ABC movie *Desperate*. He is probably best known for his role as Corky Thatcher, the star of the television series *Life Goes On*, which ran for four years. This talented actor also made guest appearances on *Touched By An Angel*, *The Promised Land*, *ER*, *The Commish*, and *The Division*. Chris starred in the television miniseries *Heaven and Hell* and in the television movie *Jonathan, the Boy Nobody Wanted*. Chris's autobiography, *A Special Kind of Hero*, made *The New York Times*'s Best Sellers list in 1992. Chris and twin brothers Joe and John DeMasi released their first folk album together in 1993. Since then, they have appeared together on numerous TV shows and toured as a folk band. Chris became friends with the DeMasi brothers when they were music counselors at the summer camp he attended as a youth.

Ruth Cromer of Australia also wanted to act. At age 11, she started drama classes. Since then, she has performed on Australian TV in a guest role on the popular series *A Country Practice* and in the *House Gang* series. She auditioned for and won a role in the play "A More Fortunate Life," with which she toured New South Wales. Ruth has also performed in videos,

FIGURE 1.1   A spokesperson and advocate for the rights of people with disabilities, actor Chris Burke starred in the television drama *Life Goes On* and also appeared in several other shows and films.

and she gives talks to schools and community groups. As a hobby, Ruth is a member of the Bondi Mermaids and the Bondi Icebergs, swimming clubs that swim throughout the year, even in winter.

Jason Kingsley began his acting career with appearances on *Sesame Street*, for which his mother was a scriptwriter. At age 10, he played a lead role in an episode of the ABC television series *The Fall Guy*. By age 23, he had been on more than 50 radio and television shows, including an episode of *Touched By an Angel*. Jason has also been the subject of more than 100 magazine and newspaper articles. In addition, he coauthored an award-winning book, *Count Us In*, with his friend, Mitchell Levitz.

What do Chris Burke, Ruth Cromer, Jason Kingsley, and Mitchell Levitz have in common? In addition to a lot of talent, they have Down syndrome. Another thing they have in common is parents who refused to accept the stereotypes about Down syndrome and who made special efforts to give their children the same opportunities that other children have. The achievements of these young people and others like them demonstrate that children with Down syndrome can participate—and even excel—in most of the same activities as their peers. To help ensure that other children with Down syndrome also receive the opportunity to reach their full potential, Chris, Ruth, Michael, and Jason serve as spokespersons and advocates for the rights of people with disabilities.

Down syndrome is a developmental disorder caused by an extra **chromosome**—a structure in the cell nucleus that contains genetic material. In the 1960s, it was not uncommon for physicians to advise parents whose babies were born with Down syndrome to place them in an institution. These parents were told that their children would never be able to hold jobs or live in mainstream society. At that time, children with Down syndrome were considered uneducable. Some infants with Down syndrome were even denied food and water, and were allowed to die.

The case of Baby Doe—a newborn with Down syndrome who died after her parents and physicians did not pursue routine surgery to fix an esophageal defect that prevented food from reaching her stomach—caught the attention of President Ronald Reagan in March of 1983. He issued federal

WILLOWBROOK

Opened in 1947, Willowbrook State School in Staten Island, N.Y., was the largest of the state-run institutions for developmentally disabled children. Children with autism, cerebral palsy, and Down syndrome were often sent there as infants or toddlers at the advice of their parents' physicians. Infectious diseases such as hepatitis (an infection of the liver) were rampant within the facility, which was dirty, crowded, and understaffed. Physical abuse of children by the staff was not uncommon. Between 1963 and 1966, a research study was conducted in which healthy children entering the facility were intentionally infected with live hepatitis virus and then monitored to gauge the effects of gamma globulin injections protecting the children from infection. During this period, the institution would admit only children whose parents allowed them to participate in such studies.

After visiting the facility in 1965, Senator Robert F. Kennedy called it a "snake pit." In late 1971, the *Staten Island Register* and the *Staten Island Advance* each published a series of articles about the deplorable conditions at Willowbrook. What really caught the public's attention, though, was a documentary rulings to prevent the recurrence of such a situation, but these were struck down in court. However, the Child Abuse Amendments of 1984, which passed while Reagan was in office, extended the Federal Child Abuse Act to include the denial of treatment and nourishment to newborns with disabilities. Yet as late as 1989, the U.S. Civil Rights Committee reported continued widespread violations of these laws and asked for further investigations.

filmed by Geraldo Rivera in January 1972. Prior to that time, photography was prohibited within the facility, even by parents who came to visit their children. Using a key provided by a young doctor who had quit his job at the facility in protest, Rivera and his camera crew charged through the gate of the facility and entered Ward 6 with their camera rolling. That night on TV, Rivera began a campaign to inform the public of the wretched conditions at the facility and to call for changes.

A class action lawsuit was filed against the state of New York by volunteer organizations, parents of Willowbrook children, and some of the residents of Willowbrook, which resulted in the Willowbrook Consent Decree of 1975, a law that obligated New York State to provide appropriate housing and programs for individuals at the institution. National reforms on the care and housing of the developmentally disabled followed. Congress passed a number of measures that protected the rights of people with disabilities. After downsizing and changing its name to Staten Island Developmental Center, Willowbrook finally closed its doors in 1987.

DOWN SYNDROME IN HISTORY

Ancient cultures, such as those in Greece, Rome, and Egypt, put disabled infants to death. Compassion toward the disabled was awakened by the early Christian church, but its charitable influence waned during the Middle Ages. During that time, intellectually disabled people were abandoned or used as jesters, the Middle Ages equivalent of a clown. Many abandoned children were given to monasteries to be cared for, a practice that decreased from the thirteenth century to the sixteenth century, by which time most abandoned children were placed in "foundling hospitals," institutions for abandoned children. It was not until the Renaissance that a humanitarian attitude again began to emerge.

During the nineteenth century, concern about the welfare of people with intellectual disabilities spread to the medical establishment. Before that time, care of the intellectually disabled had been the responsibility of monks and empathetic neighbors. In his 1838 book, which is considered the first psychiatry handbook, French physician Jean-Etienne-Dominique Esquirol described a patient category with the physical characteristics of what is now known as Down syndrome. French physician Edouard Séguin expanded Esquirol's description with additional details in 1846 and considered the condition to be a type of cretinism. Cretinism is a disorder caused by **hypothyroidism** that results from problems with the thyroid gland or a lack of iodine. Left untreated, cretinism results in small stature and mental retardation. In 1866, English physician John Langdon Down became the first person to categorize Down syndrome as a specific disorder.

Scientists have wondered why there is no written history of Down syndrome as a specific disease before its categorization by John Langdon Down in 1866. Some, such as Swiss-

American physician Hans Zellweger and British physician B.W. Richards have speculated that Down syndrome is a modern disease because it was rare before the nineteenth century. Among the hypotheses that have been formulated to account for this supposed rarity are shorter life expectancy of mothers and the high rate of infant mortality before the nineteenth century. Older mothers are more likely to have children with Down syndrome. Without the advantages of modern medicine, children with Down syndrome would have been more likely to die during infancy or early childhood. Alternatively, Peter Volpe, a professor at Mercer University School of Medicine, thinks the lack of mention of Down syndrome is primarily because it was considered a subcategory of cretinism and therefore was simply not recognized as a specific disorder.

There is also very little representation of Down syndrome in art over the centuries. Only a few paintings, such as the sixteenth century Flemish painting *The Adoration of the Christ Child,* have been identified in which characters appear to have facial features and other characteristics typical of Down syndrome. Cretins, however, were recognized in literature and art long before the nineteenth century. Cretinism was especially common in certain inland areas, such as the Swiss Alps, where the soil content of iodine was low.

Probably the first evidence of Down syndrome can be found in pottery fragments discovered in South America. People of the Tumaco-La Tolita culture inhabited the borders of what is now Ecuador and Colombia for about 1,000 years and disappeared before the arrival of Spanish explorers. They left a large collection of figurines and pottery that very realistically depicted all aspects of life, from figures showing everyday life and emotions to those with physical disabilities. Several of these figurines display physical features characteristic of Down syndrome. A terra cotta figure of an infant with Down syndrome that was crafted around AD 500 is considered the oldest historical evidence of the disorder.

PHYSICAL CHARACTERISTICS OF DOWN SYNDROME

Before genetic testing became available, Down syndrome was diagnosed based on certain typical physical characteristics. However, not all individuals with Down syndrome have all of these characteristics, which vary with the individual and are caused by the extra chromosome.

An infant with Down syndrome usually has low muscle tone and poor reflexes. The joints are looser than normal. The skull is somewhat short and broad and slightly smaller, and the back of the head flatter, than normal. Fontanelles (or "soft spots"), structures on a baby's head that usually close by 2 years of age, are typically larger and close later than in babies developing normally. There may be three of these instead of the usual two. Newborns with Down syndrome often have extra skin on the back of the neck. As the child gets older, the neck often appears short and wider than usual.

Facial shape is round in the newborn and during infancy. As the child ages, his or her facial shape becomes more oval. Due to underdevelopment, the middle of the face appears flat. The nose is small, and the nasal bridge is flatter than normal. The nares, or nasal openings, are usually small. Nasal passages may be narrower, which causes them to become congested more easily. The cheeks are round, and the mouth may be small and have corners that are turned down. Low muscle tone and a small oral cavity may cause the tongue to protrude. The teeth, which develop late and in an unusual order, may be small and unusually shaped.

FIGURE 1.2 An epicanthal fold is a fold of skin from the upper eyelid that covers the inside corner of the eye. Epicanthal folds are found in people of Asian descent and in young children. They are found more frequently in children with Down syndrome than in the general population.

The **palpebral fissures,** or openings of the eyes, are smaller than normal and slanted upward. **Brushfield spots,** or small white spots on the iris, are characteristic. Small folds of skin, called **epicanthal folds,** cover the inner corners of the eyes. Because of this characteristic, John Langdon Down named the disorder "mongolism," a term that was later deemed inappropriate and replaced first by "Down's syndrome" in 1961 and eventually by "Down syndrome."

The ears of individuals with Down syndrome tend to be small, and they may be slightly lower on the head than usual. They may be cupped, or the upper part may fold over, producing a somewhat square shape. Ear passages may be smaller and more easily blocked, which can cause hearing loss if not treated.

Individuals with Down syndrome tend to be shorter and stockier than individuals in the general population. The hands may be wide and short, with fingers that are shorter than normal. The fifth finger may curve inward and have one crease instead of two. About half of individuals with Down syndrome have one deep **palmar crease** (a crease across the palm) instead of the usual two. The feet tend to be wide

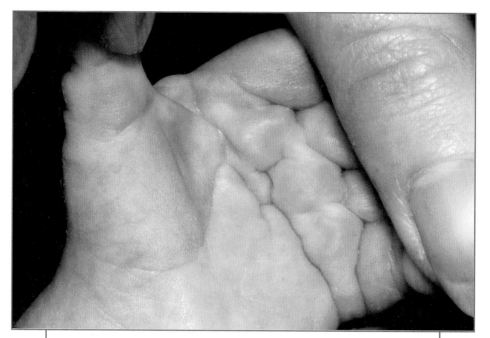

FIGURE 1.3   Individuals with Down syndrome often have a single crease across the palm of the hand instead of the usual two. Called a simian crease, or a transverse palmar crease, this characteristic is found in 1 out of 30 people who do not have Down syndrome.

and short, often with a characteristic gap between the first two toes. If this gap is present, a **plantar crease** (a deep crease in the bottom of the foot) will extend from the gap.

INCIDENCE OF DOWN SYNDROME

Recent statistics from various U.S. and European studies place the incidence of Down syndrome anywhere from 1 in 600 to 1 in 1,000 live births. An analysis published by I. Bray and colleagues in 1998 of combined data from nine different studies found that the incidence varies from 1 in 1,445 live births to mothers at age 20 to 1 in 25 live births to mothers at age 45. The increased incidence in older mothers is because of errors in reproductive cell division that may result from age-related changes in the egg precursor cells, which are all present at the mother's birth. About 1 in 150 miscarriages during the first 3 months of pregnancy are due to Down syndrome. Miscarriages also occur in about 35% of pregnancies in which Down syndrome is diagnosed between 15 and 28 weeks of pregnancy. Some of these miscarriages may be caused by prenatal screening procedures, which carry a risk of miscarriage.

LIFE EXPECTANCY WITH DOWN SYNDROME

Advances in medical treatment over the past 40 to 50 years for conditions such as heart defects and respiratory disease have led to dramatic increases in the life expectancy of individuals with Down syndrome. Approximately half of the children born with Down syndrome during the early 1960s survived to age 5. Bronchopneumonia, a respiratory illness, and heart defects were the most common causes of death. Now about 80% of those born with Down syndrome survive to age 10, and about 50% survive to age 50 or beyond.

The physical characteristics described in this chapter represent just one aspect of the challenges faced by individuals with Down syndrome. The following chapters will further examine not only the physical and intellectual challenges faced by individuals with Down syndrome, but also social challenges and how they can create obstacles to obtaining equal opportunities in education and employment. To understand how an extra chromosome can affect the development of individuals with Down syndrome, the following chapters will discuss genetic principles and techniques, and also explore the medical advances and treatment interventions that have enabled people such as Chris Burke, Ruth Cromer, Mitchell Levitz, and Jason Kingsley to shatter stereotypes about Down syndrome.

2

DNA: BLUEPRINT
FOR LIFE

The science of genetics had obscure beginnings in the monastery garden of Gregor Mendel, an Austrian monk who spent eight years studying the inheritance characteristics of the common garden pea plant. Mendel cross-pollinated purebred strains of these plants and did a mathematical analysis of how certain traits such as flower color and seed shape were transmitted to offspring. The principles of heredity that he discovered would one day become known as Mendel's laws, and he would become known as the "father of genetics." However, his results, which were published in 1866, would go relatively unnoticed for 34 more years.

In 1900, Mendel's work was rediscovered by Dutch botanist Hugo de Vries and German botanist Carl Correns. The significance of Mendel's discoveries, which had not been understood by the scientists of his own time, was finally realized. The next major step in the new field was for scientists to understand the biological basis for the transmission of traits from parents to offspring. In 1902, Walter S. Sutton demonstrated that chromosomes occur in definite pairs as opposed to being a single continuous thread, as popularly thought. He further suggested that the separation of chromosomes during cell division might be the mechanism by which Mendelian inheritance occurred.

Units of inheritance called **genes** were thought to be located on the chromosomes. It was not until the 1950s, however, that the chemical nature of the gene was fully established. Nucleic acids had been extracted from white blood cell nuclei by Swiss biologist Friedrich Miescher in 1869 and were at first believed to be the principal material of which chromosomes were made. By 1925, however, scientists had incorrectly concluded that genes were made of proteins instead, and it was not until 1945 that attention was again focused on nucleic acids as potential hereditary material.

Work in bacteria by the research team of Oswald T. Avery at the Rockefeller Institute in New York City culminated in a paper in 1944 that established the importance of **deoxyribonucleic acid (DNA)** in heredity. However, it was not yet known how the seemingly repetitive structure of DNA could contain the information for the many genes involved in hereditary transmission. Building on biochemist Linus Pauling's discovery in 1951 that the protein molecule is coiled in a form known as the alpha helix, James Watson and Francis Crick announced their discovery of the **double helix** structure of DNA in 1953. Pauling himself had speculated in 1946 that the gene might be composed of two **complementary** strands of DNA. With Watson's and Crick's discovery of the double helix, the field of molecular genetics was launched. Major discoveries were still ahead, as scientists tried to figure out how genes do their job and how to decipher the genetic code found in the DNA molecule.

CHROMATIN

Scientists today know that the nucleus of every cell in the body contains a blueprint for life. This blueprint is found in the genetic code of the DNA molecule. In cells that are not dividing, threadlike strands of **chromatin** can be seen in the cell nucleus. Chromatin is a complex of DNA and the proteins around which it wraps. This wrapping of the DNA allows it to fit inside the tiny cell nucleus. If all of the DNA in

FRUIT FLY GENETICS

To understand complex processes in humans, scientists often study simpler organisms, such as the fruit fly, nematode (roundworm), or housefly. Many of the basic processes and organ systems of humans are present in these organisms, albeit in much simpler forms. The fruit fly *Drosophila melanogaster* has been especially important in the study of genetics.

Geneticist Thomas Hunt Morgan conducted the first important research with the fruit fly. He and his research team made a number of important discoveries about the laws of heredity. Because the short life cycle of *Drosophila* allows the production of many generations in a short time, Morgan's team was able to discover a number of **mutations.** Cross-breeding experiments allowed them to establish relationships between the mutations that led them to the conclusion that genes were located on chromosomes. In 1933, Morgan was awarded the Nobel Prize for his discoveries about the role of the chromosomes in heredity.

Since 50% of *Drosophila* genes have human counterparts, including 61% of the genes known to be important in human disease, research is also being done with *Drosophila* in areas such as Parkinson's disease, diabetes, and birth defects. In 1946, fruit flies became the first animals in space when they were sent up inside a V2 rocket to assess radiation effects. Since then, fruit flies have been regular research participants during space missions and have helped answer questions about such things as the effect of microgravity on the immune system.

a single cell were placed end to end, it would form a strand 3 meters long, about the length of a car.

THE GENETIC CODE

The DNA molecule is made of two cross-linked strands of DNA and looks somewhat like a twisted ladder or a spiral staircase (Figure 2.1). Molecules of deoxyribose (a sugar with five carbon atoms) and phosphate (made of phosphorus and oxygen) alternate to form each side of this ladder and are held together by strong chemical bonds. Each sugar molecule binds to one of four nitrogen bases: cytosine, thymine, adenine, or guanine. This nitrogen base is in turn connected by a weak hydrogen bond to the base opposite it on the other strand of the DNA ladder.

A **nucleotide** is a subunit of DNA composed of one base, one deoxyribose, and one phosphate. For convenience, each nucleotide is referred to by the first letter of its base: A for adenine, G for guanine, C for cytosine, and T for thymine. There are 3 billion nucleotide pairs in the human genome, which consists of all the DNA of all the chromosomes. It is the nucleotide sequence found in DNA that constitutes the genetic code, a code that was finally deciphered amid a lot of excitement during the 1960s.

A triplet of nucleotides that is specific for a particular amino acid is called a **codon**. Each protein is encoded by a specific sequence of codons. All together, there are 64

(opposite) **FIGURE 2.1**   Each rung of the DNA ladder is composed of a pair of nitrogen bases: either cytosine and thymine, or adenine and guanine. Cytosine is always paired with thymine, and adenine is always paired with guanine. Nucleotides in a sequence, which form the sides of the DNA ladder, are bound together by a chemical bond between the phosphate molecule of one nucleotide and the sugar molecule of the adjacent nucleotide.

codons and 20 different **amino acids**. Therefore, the number of different codons that represent a particular amino acid ranges from one codon for methionine (ATG) and

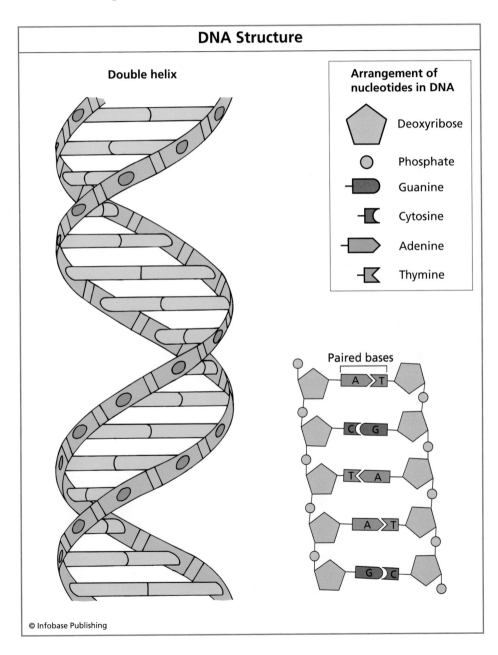

DNA Structure

Double helix

Arrangement of nucleotides in DNA

⬠ Deoxyribose

○ Phosphate

Guanine

Cytosine

Adenine

Thymine

Paired bases

A — T

C — G

T — A

A — T

G — C

tryptophan (TGG) to six codons for leucine, serine, and arginine (Figure 2.2). If nucleotide bases can be thought of as letters in the alphabet, then codons can be thought of as words. There are special start and stop codons before and after the codon sequence for each protein.

A codon sequence that represents the amino acid sequence of a protein is called a gene. (Proteins, the final product of **gene expression,** range in size from 40 to 50 amino acids to several thousand amino acids, with an average of about 300.) All together, there are about 20,000 to 25,000 genes,

DNA Codons for Amino Acids

First Position of Codon	Second Position of Codon				Third Position of Codon
	T	**C**	**A**	**G**	
T	TTT Phe (F)	TCT Ser (S)	TAT Tyr (Y)	TGT Cys (C)	T
	TTC Phe (F)	TCC Ser (S)	TAC Tyr (Y)	TGC Cys (C)	C
	TTA Leu (L)	TCA Ser (S)	TAA Ter (end)	TGA Ter (end)	A
	TTG Leu (L)	TCG Ser (S)	TAG Ter (end)	TGG Trp (W)	G
C	CTT Leu (L)	CCT Pro (P)	CAT His (H)	CGT Arg (R)	T
	CTC Leu (L)	CCC Pro (P)	CAC His (H)	CGC Arg (R)	C
	CTA Leu (L)	CCA Pro (P)	CAA Gln (Q)	CGA Arg (R)	A
	CTG Leu (L)	CCG Pro (P)	CAG Gln (Q)	CGG Arg (R)	G
A	ATT De (I)	ACT Thr (T)	AAT Asn (N)	AGT Ser (S)	T
	ATC De (I)	ACC Thr (T)	AAC Asn (N)	AGC Ser (S)	C
	ATA De (I)	ACA Thr (T)	AAA Lys (K)	AGA Arg (R)	A
	ATG Met (M)	ACG Thr (T)	AAG Lys (K)	AGG Arg (R)	G
G	GTT Val (V)	GCT Ala (A)	GAT Asp (D)	GGT Gly (G)	T
	GTC Val (V)	GCC Ala (A)	GAC Asp (D)	GGC Gly (G)	C
	GTA Val (V)	GCA Ala (A)	GAA Glu (E)	GGA Gly (G)	A
	GTG Val (V)	GCG Ala (A)	GAG Glu (E)	GGG Gly (G)	G

© Infobase Publishing

FIGURE 2.2 This chart illustrates the codons formed by all possible arrangements of the three nitrogenous bases of the DNA molecule. Also shown are the abbreviations of the amino acids that are specified by the various codons.

which make up less than 5% of the total DNA in the human genome. Except for regulatory sequences that control the expression of genes into proteins, the function of the remainder of **DNA sequences** is still not completely understood.

CHROMOSOMES

Humans have 23 pairs of chromosomes in their cells. Various species of plants and animals have different numbers of chromosome pairs. For example, a cat has 19 pairs, a guinea pig has 32 pairs, a petunia has 7 pairs, and a camel has 35 pairs. Each member of a pair of chromosomes contains genes that help control the expression of the same traits. A gene may occur in two or more forms, called alleles. The allele of a particular gene found on one chromosome of a pair may be identical or different to the allele found on the other chromosome. For example, one chromosome of a pair may contain the allele for blue eye color and the other may contain an allele for blue eye color.

MITOSIS AND MEIOSIS

Most cells of the body divide through a process called **mitosis,** in which two daughter cells that have the same number of chromosome pairs as the original cell are produced. This type of cell division allows for growth and replacement of cells. A different type of cell division, called **meiosis,** occurs in reproductive cells. Egg and sperm cells, which are the end result of meiotic cell divisions, contain only half the number of chromosomes as other cells. In other words, they each contain 23 individual chromosomes instead of 23 pairs of chromosomes. When their chromosomes are combined after fertilization, the zygote, or fertilized cell,

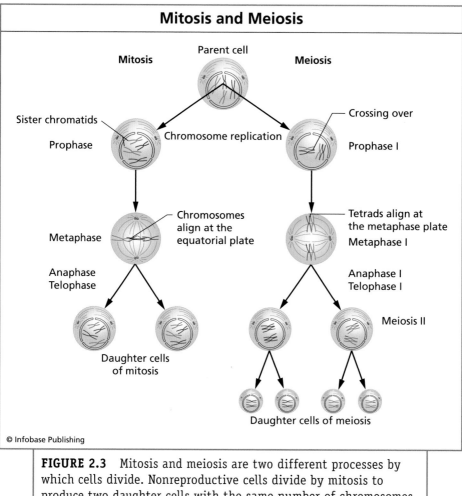

Mitosis and Meiosis

FIGURE 2.3 Mitosis and meiosis are two different processes by which cells divide. Nonreproductive cells divide by mitosis to produce two daughter cells with the same number of chromosomes as the parent cell. Reproductive cells divide by meiosis to produce four daughter cells that have half the number of chromosomes as the nonreproductive cells.

that results and develops into an embryo has the usual 23 pairs of chromosomes. Otherwise, each new generation would have double the number of chromosomes of the previous generation. The process of meiosis prevents this from happening.

Mitosis

Mitosis occurs in five stages, or phases. **Interphase** is the phase between cell division, when the chromatin is thread-like in appearance. During interphase, the chromosomes duplicate, and then one of each pair moves to opposite ends of the cell during prophase. At the same time, the chromosomes become denser and more compact as the DNA molecules wrap more tightly around the proteins with which they are associated. Each duplicated chromosome now consists of a pair of sister chromatids. During metaphase, the chromatids line up across the center, or equator, of the cell. They separate during anaphase and move toward opposite poles of the cell. When the new chromosomes have completed their journey, telophase begins, and the chromosomes uncoil. Nuclear membranes form around the two sets of chromosomes, so that the cell now has two nuclei. Then the cytoplasm of the cell divides so that there are now two new cells, each of which contains the original number of chromosomes.

Meiosis

There are two stages in meiosis, called Meiosis I and Meiosis II. Each consists of five stages similar to, but different in important ways, from the five stages of mitosis. The chromosomes duplicate during interphase I as they did in mitosis. What is different in prophase I is that the members of each pair of chromosomes line up together in a bundle of four chromatids that is called a tetrad. Whereas the chromosomes line up individually during mitosis, the chromosomes line up as pairs during Metaphase I. During Anaphase I, one chromosome from each pair moves toward each pole. (One chromatid from each chromosome moves toward each pole in mitosis.) Formation of new nuclear membranes and division of the cytoplasm occurs during Telophase I. During Interphase II, the chromosomes do not duplicate. The chromosomes condense during Prophase II and then line up at the center of the cell during Metaphase II. One chromatid from each chromosome moves to each pole during Anaphase II. New nuclear membranes are formed, and the cytoplasm divides during Telophase II. The two divisions of Meiosis result in the production of four cells, each with half the number of chromosomes found in nonreproductive cells.

DNA REPLICATION

DNA replication is the process by which a DNA molecule is duplicated during mitosis and meiosis. During this process, the two original strands of DNA are separated, and a new strand of nucleotides is added to each of the original strands. Just as the original strands were complementary to each other, each new strand is complementary to the strand on which it is

(opposite) **FIGURE 2.4**   In DNA replication, a short sequence of ribonucleic acid (RNA), called a primer, that is complementary to the nucleotide sequence to which it attaches, is synthesized by the enzyme DNA polymerase. On the leading strand, DNA nucleotides are added at the end of this primer until the new strand is completed Since the nucleotides on the opposite, or lagging strand, are oriented in the opposite direction, multiple primers are synthesized at intervals by the DNA primase enzyme. DNA polymerase then adds DNA nucleotides to the end of each primer. The discontinuous sequences formed on the lagging strand are called Okazaki fragments. After all the DNA nucleotides have been added, the RNA nucleotides of the primers are replaced with DNA nucleotides. Then the DNA ligase enzyme causes the nucleotides at the ends of adjacent Okazaki fragments to bond chemically so that the lagging strand is now complete.

synthesized. For each nucleotide on the original strand, a nucleotide containing a complementary base will be opposite it on the new strand. For example, a nucleotide containing

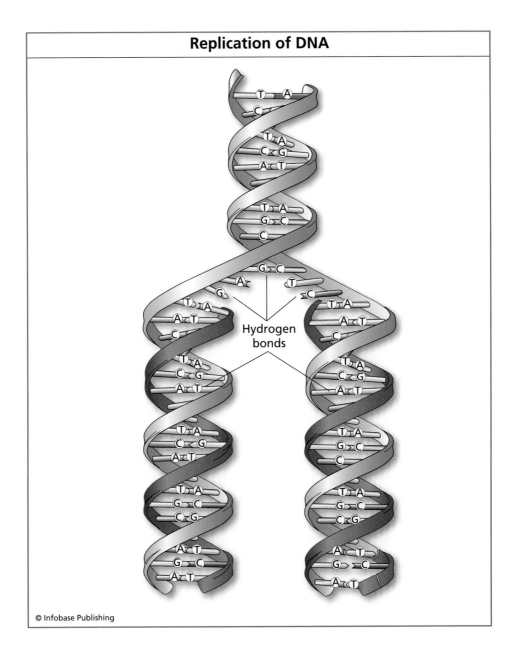

Replication of DNA

Hydrogen
bonds

adenine will always be opposite one containing thymine, and a nucleotide containing guanine will always be opposite one containing cytosine.

Since 3 billion base pairs must be replicated, this process could take a very long time. However, the entire DNA molecule does not unzip, or break apart, at one time. Instead, as many as a hundred replication "bubbles" form at different locations on the DNA molecule and begin to unzip the hydrogen bonds between base pairs. The replication bubbles continue to unzip as the new strands are replicated inside them. Eventually, all the replication bubbles meet, and the two new strands are complete. A process that would take a month at the rate of 50 base pairs added per second takes only an hour because of simultaneous replication in the replication bubbles.

DNA REPAIR

Errors in DNA are corrected by the **DNA repair** system, which detects and repairs errors made during replication as well as damage to DNA caused by byproducts of cellular processes and by environmental insults. DNA mismatch repair occurs within a few minutes of replication and catches replication errors that eluded the proofreading function of DNA polymerase. It reduces the occurrence of mutations in the DNA molecule and is an important factor in the low error rate of DNA replication. Damage to DNA after replication is repaired by two methods. Direct reversal of damage by chemical means restores damaged base(s) to their original state. **Excision repair** involves removing and replacing a damaged base or nucleotide.

3

GENE EXPRESSION

Once the zygote is formed and the embryo begins to develop, the genetic blueprint must be used to form structures that carry out life processes. Throughout life, each cell of the body depends on the genetic code contained within its nucleus to direct its activities. For this to happen, the genetic code must be communicated from the nucleus to the rest of the cell. This is done when a molecule called messenger ribonucleic acid (mRNA) is formed through a process called **transcription.** Each mRNA molecule is a copy, or **transcript,** of the nucleotide sequence for a particular gene.

TRANSCRIPTION

For transcription to begin, one or more **transcription factors** must bind to the DNA at a promoter region, a site adjacent to the nucleotide sequence of a particular gene. About 10% of the genes code for these proteins, which regulate the expression of other proteins by increasing or decreasing their transcription. Once the transcription factors have identified the starting point for transcription, RNA

DNA Transcription

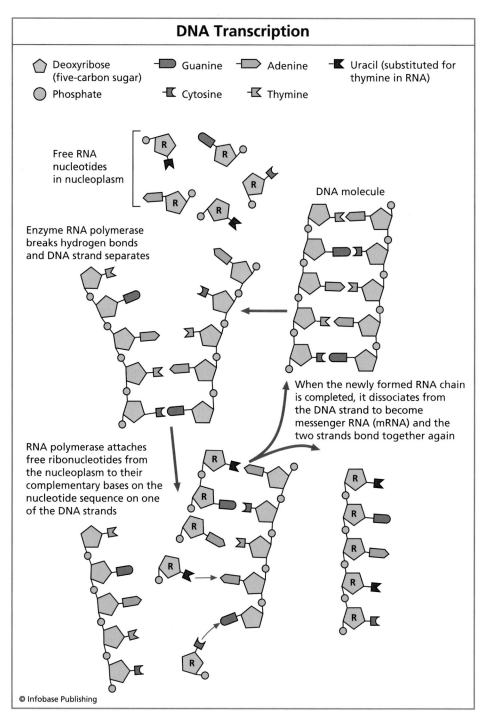

Deoxyribose (five-carbon sugar)

Phosphate

Guanine

Cytosine

Adenine

Thymine

Uracil (substituted for thymine in RNA)

Free RNA nucleotides in nucleoplasm

DNA molecule

Enzyme RNA polymerase breaks hydrogen bonds and DNA strand separates

When the newly formed RNA chain is completed, it dissociates from the DNA strand to become messenger RNA (mRNA) and the two strands bond together again

RNA polymerase attaches free ribonucleotides from the nucleoplasm to their complementary bases on the nucleotide sequence on one of the DNA strands

© Infobase Publishing

polymerase binds to the promoter region, unwinds a portion of the DNA double helix to begin a transcription bubble. As it moves down the nucleotide sequence of the gene it is transcribing, RNA polymerase assembles a complementary strand of RNA nucleotides. When the strand is completed, it detaches from the RNA polymerase as the mRNA transcript of the gene.

For any particular gene, the same strand of the DNA molecule is always used as the template strand for making the RNA transcript. The nucleotides of the mRNA transcript are complementary to the template strand being copied, and they are identical to those of the nontemplate strand, with two important differences. One difference is that the mRNA molecule contains the nucleotide uracil instead of thymine. The other difference is that the sugar molecule of the RNA nucleotide is different. Ribose is the sugar molecule found in ribonucleic acid (RNA) nucleotides; deoxyribose is the sugar molecule present in DNA nucleotides. Deoxyribose is identical to ribose except that it has one less hydroxyl (oxygen-hydrogen) group.

TRANSLATION

Once the mRNA transcript is in its final form, it moves through a pore in the nuclear membrane into the **cytoplasm**—the cell material outside the nucleus. In

---

(opposite) **FIGURE 3.1**   Transcription is regulated by transcription factors, which identify the starting point for transcription of a gene. RNA polymerase interacts with the transcription factors to unwind the DNA and then assembles a strand of ribonucleotides that is complementary to the nucleotide sequence of the gene that is being transcribed.

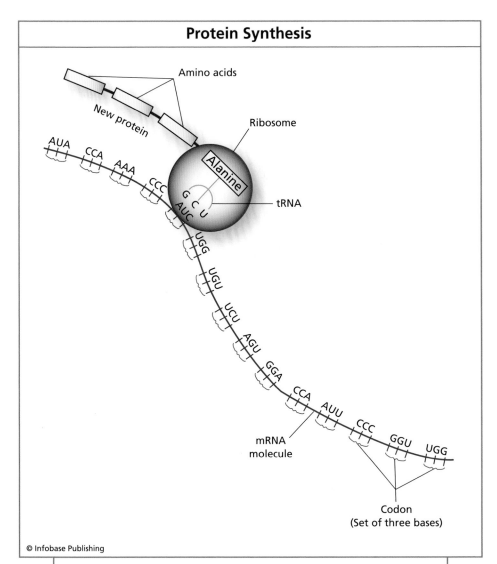

Protein Synthesis

Amino acids

New protein

Ribosome

AUA CCA AAA CCC

Alanine

G C U
AUC

tRNA

UGG

UGU

UCU

AGU

GGA

CCA

AUU

CCC

GGU UGG

mRNA
molecule

Codon
(Set of three bases)

© Infobase Publishing

FIGURE 3.2   As a ribosome reads each codon on the mRNA transcript, the amino acid specified by that nucleotide sequence is brought to the ribosome and added to the polypeptide chain being built. Another type of RNA, **transfer RNA (tRNA)** transfers amino acids from the cytoplasm to the ribosome to be assembled into polypeptides. There is at least one specific tRNA for each of the 20 amino acids from which polypeptides are built. After the polypeptide is complete, the mRNA transcript and the polypeptide are released from the ribosome.

the cytoplasm, the nucleotide sequence of the mRNA transcript is used to build the polypeptide for which it codes. The term **peptide** refers to two or more amino acids that are linked together. A polypeptide is a chain of amino acids. Proteins are made of one or more polypeptides.

MITOCHONDRIAL DNA

Mitochondria are tiny organelles found in the cytoplasm that produce the energy that each cell needs. There may be hundreds of mitochondria in the most active cells. Energy stored in carbohydrates and fats is converted by mitochondria into the molecule adenosine triphosphate (ATP), which provides energy for the many biochemical reactions within the cell. Mitochondria and the chloroplasts of photosynthetic plants are unique in that they each have their own DNA molecule (of which there may be multiple copies) that is not part of the nuclear chromosomes. (Chloroplasts are chlorophyll-containing plant organelles that, when stimulated by light, synthesize sugar from carbon dioxide and water.)

Human mitochondria contain a circular, double-stranded DNA molecule called mitochondrial DNA (mtDNA), which is 16,659 nucleotides long and encodes for 37 genes that have no **introns**, or parts of genes that do not code for proteins. Of these genes, 13 code for proteins involved in the process by which ATP is made, 22 code for transfer RNAs, and 2 code for rRNAs. Mitochondria transcribe and translate their own DNA into proteins specific for their energy-producing function. Mitochondrial ribosomal proteins and many of the proteins involved in the production of ATP are encoded by genes in nuclear DNA and synthesized in the cytoplasm. There is therefore some interplay between gene products of mitochondrial and nuclear DNA.

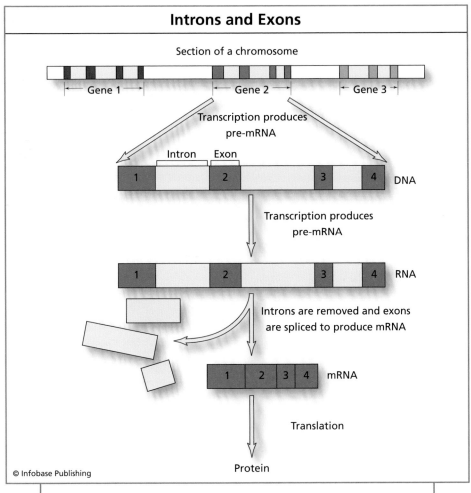

Introns and Exons

Section of a chromosome

Gene 1 — Gene 2 — Gene 3

Transcription produces
pre-mRNA

Intron   Exon

1   2   3   4   DNA

Transcription produces
pre-mRNA

1   2   3   4   RNA

Introns are removed and exons
are spliced to produce mRNA

1 2 3 4   mRNA

Translation

Protein

© Infobase Publishing

FIGURE 3.3 The initial mRNA transcript undergoes further processing. There are noncoding sequences called introns that must be spliced, or cut out of the pre-mRNA molecule. Their function, if any, has not yet been determined. The coding sequences that remain after the introns are removed are called exons.

Translation is the term used for the process by which the mRNA transcript of the nucleotide sequence of a gene is used to determine the amino acid sequence of the polypeptide for which it codes. A complex of protein and RNA molecules called a **ribosome** is the site where the translation of mRNA into protein occurs; the type of RNA found in ribosomes is called ribosomal RNA (rRNA). Numerous ribosomes are present in the cytoplasm, and many are found on the endoplasmic reticulum, an **organelle** that forms a network of membranes in the cytoplasm.

TYPES OF PROTEINS

One way that proteins can be classified is by their function. **Structural proteins,** as their name implies, form the structures of the body. Keratin (found in skin, hair, and nails) and collagen (found in skin, bone, teeth, and connective tissues) are examples of structural proteins. **Transport proteins** include the hemoglobin molecule, which carries oxygen through the blood. Other examples of transport proteins include proteins that are embedded in the cell membrane and regulate the passage of nutrients into the cell and the movement of ions into and out of the cell. **Enzymes** are proteins that catalyze chemical reactions in the cell by bringing substances together and causing them to react while remaining unchanged by the reaction. **Regulatory proteins** include **transcription factors,** which regulate the expression of genes by the cell. Other examples of regulatory proteins are hormones and their receptors, enzymes involved in blood clotting, and signaling molecules that transmit signals from the cell membrane to the nucleus or to the cytoplasm.

4

GENETIC DISEASES

A change in just one amino acid can inactivate a protein and cause a reduction in or loss of its function. For example, sickle cell anemia is caused by the substitution of thymine for adenine in just one codon of the gene for hemoglobin. This results in the substitution of the amino acid valine (GAG) for glutamine (GTG) at that position in the hemoglobin molecule. Cystic fibrosis is caused by the deletion of the amino acid phenylalanine at one position on a chloride ion channel protein. The defective ion channel protein is destroyed by the cell, and its absence causes the symptoms of cystic fibrosis.

A disease caused by deficient activity of an enzyme in a metabolic pathway is called a **metabolic error.** Phenylketonuria, a metabolic disorder in which the amino acid phenylalanine is not metabolized properly, results in mental retardation unless infants with two defective copies of the gene for the phenylalanine hydroxylase enzyme are started on a low-phenylalanine diet soon after birth. Albinism, in which the skin pigment melanin is not produced, is caused by deficient activity of the enzyme tyrosinase, which is involved in the synthesis of melanin.

FIGURE 4.1   Discovered in equatorial Guinea in 1966, Snowflake was the only known albino gorilla. Snowflake became the most popular resident at the Barcelona zoo in Spain, where he lived for 37 years.

MUTATIONS

Changes in the genetic material that result from mistakes during replication or damage to the DNA molecule are called mutations. Point mutations are changes in a gene caused by an incorrect base pair or the deletion or insertion of nucleotide pairs. Many gene mutations provide genetic variability without doing harm to the organism. However, some gene mutations result in illness or death.

Spontaneous mutations are those for which we do not know the cause. They may result from replication errors that were not detected by the DNA repair system. Or they may be caused by products of cellular metabolism, such as free radicals. A free radical is an ion, atom, or molecule that has an electron in its outer shell that is not paired with another electron. This makes it highly reactive, causing it to steal an electron from a nearby molecule or compound. This can result in a chain reaction, with a new free radical being formed at each step. Free radicals are thought to cause damage to DNA, cellular proteins, and the cell membrane. If this damage accumulates over time, it can cause disease and may be a component of the aging process. Antioxidants such as vitamin C neutralize free radicals by giving them the electron needed to stabilize them.

Induced mutations are caused by **mutagens,** which are chemical or physical agents in the environment. Mutagens include certain types of radiation, food components, certain plant toxins, chemotherapy agents, and some environmental chemicals. Ultraviolet light, X-rays, and gamma rays, as well as radioactive elements found in rocks and soil, cosmic rays from outer space, and radon in the atmosphere are mutagens. Heterocyclic amines produced when meats are grilled, broiled, or fried are mutagenic, as is nitrous acid formed by digestion of nitrite preservatives. One mutagen found in plants is aflatoxin B1, a fungal toxin that was originally discovered in peanuts but is also found on other plants, such as corn and tobacco. Hundreds of chemicals used in the laboratory or in industry are mutagens. Examples are nitrogen mustard (a component of mustard gas), some of the hydrocarbons in tobacco smoke, certain dyes and markers used in laboratory procedures, the preservative formaldehyde, hydrogen peroxide, the pesticide DDT, saccharin, and sodium nitrite.

MITOCHONDRIAL GENETIC DISORDERS

When a sperm and egg unite, the egg contributes most of the zygote's cytoplasm and, consequently, essentially all of its cytoplasmic organelles. Mitochondrial DNA is therefore passed to each child by its mother. Mutations in mtDNA are thus passed to offspring only through the mother, just like mutations on the Y (male) chromosome are passed to male offspring only through the father. Leber's hereditary optic neuropathy (LHON), a disease that results in sudden blindness, is an example of disease caused by an mtDNA mutation. Like other mitochondrial genetic disorders, LHON is transmitted only through females.

ANEUPLOIDY

Chromosome mutations are mutations that cause changes in the structure or number of chromosomes. **Euploidy** is a change in the number of complete sets of the genome, whereas **aneuploidy** is a change in the number of one or more pairs of chromosomes. In human fetuses, euploidy is incompatible with survival, as is aneuploidy for most

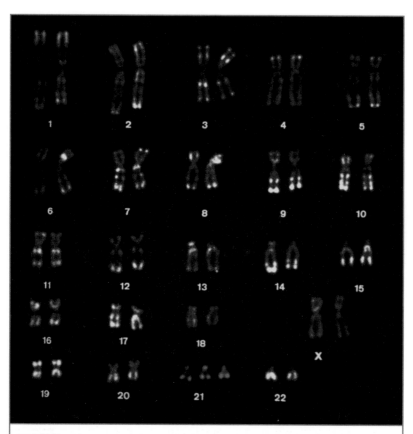

FIGURE 4.2 As seen in this karyotype, in which the chromosome pairs are identified, an individual with Down syndrome has 3 copies of Chromosome 21. It is thought that this extra genetic material is responsible for many of the physical characteristics and health issues that are seen more frequently in people with Down syndrome.

chromosome pairs. However, there are several aneuploid conditions with an extra chromosome that can result in a live birth. The most common among these is Down syndrome, in which an extra copy of chromosome 21 is present. An extra set of either sex chromosome also results in live births and allows the individual to survive into adulthood. An extra copy of chromosome 13 or 18 can result in a live birth, but results in death within a few weeks for children born with an extra chromosome 18 or a few months for a child born with an extra chromosome 13. All other aneuploidies produce conditions in which the fetus dies before birth.

Failure of chromosomes to pair or separate properly during either Meiosis I or Meiosis II can result in both chromosomes of a pair going to the same pole of the cell. This is called **nondisjunction,** which results in the mature egg or sperm cell having either one or three copies of a chromosome instead of the usual two copies. **Monosomy,** a type of aneuploidy in which only one copy of a particular chromosome is present, results in very few live births. As noted above, live births are seen with greater frequency with **trisomy,** a type of aneuploidy in which three copies of a particular chromosome are present.

TRISOMY 21

Trisomy 21 is a condition in which chromosome 21 occurs in triplicate. It was discovered independently in 1959 by French geneticist Jérôme Lejeune and British researcher Patricia Jacobs that trisomy 21 produces the developmental differences seen in Down syndrome. Most individuals with Down syndrome have 47 chromosomes instead of 46, due to the presence of an extra copy of the smallest chromosome. This aneuploidy occurs in 0.15% of the general population but occurs 2% of the time when women 45 years and older give birth. About 90% to 95 % of chromosome 21 nondisjunctions occur during egg formation, and the other 5% to 10% occur during sperm formation. About half of all nondisjunctions occur during meiosis 1. Nondisjunction is the cause of about 95% of Down syndrome cases.

TRANSLOCATION

Chomosomal rearrangement, also known as **translocation,** can result from breaks in both strands of the DNA molecule at two or more locations. Unless repaired, these breaks could be lethal. If the DNA repair system rejoins the broken

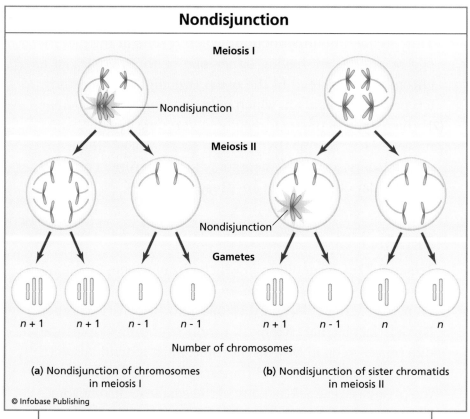

Nondisjunction

Meiosis I

Nondisjunction

Meiosis II

Nondisjunction

Gametes

$n+1$ $n+1$ $n-1$ $n-1$ $n+1$ $n-1$ n n

Number of chromosomes

(a) Nondisjunction of chromosomes in meiosis I

(b) Nondisjunction of sister chromatids in meiosis II

© Infobase Publishing

FIGURE 4.3 Figure A illustrates nondisjunction during meiosis. If fertilization occurs, cells with one more chromosome than usual will produce a zygote with a trisomy. Cells with one less chromosome than normal will not usually result in a live birth.

Figure B illustrates nondisjunction during mitosis following normal disjunction during meiosis. As a result, some tissues will have cells with 3 copies of chromosome 21, and other tissues will have cells with 2 copies.

Crossing Over

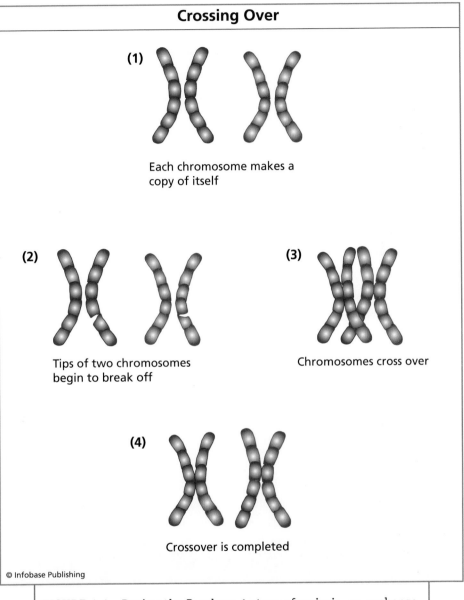

(1) Each chromosome makes a copy of itself

(2) Tips of two chromosomes begin to break off

(3) Chromosomes cross over

(4) Crossover is completed

© Infobase Publishing

FIGURE 4.4   During the Prophase 1 stage of meiosis, an exchange of DNA sequences occurs between the two nonsister chromatids of a chromosome pair in a process called crossing over. This exchange of genes is also called genetic recombination. This process allows more variability in inherited traits.

ends correctly, the DNA sequence is unchanged. However, if the broken ends are joined at a different place on the chromosome or on another chromosome, a chromosomal rearrangement occurs.

WHAT IS MOSAICISM?

Mosaicism occurs when an aneuploidy is present in some cells or tissues but not others. There are two ways in which mosaicism can occur in Down syndrome. In about 70% of mosaic Down syndrome cases, the zygote has 47 chromosomes. However, as the embryo develops from the zygote through mitotic cell divisions, a second nondisjunction occurs in one or more cells. As a result, some embryonic cells will have trisomy 21 and some will not. In the other 30% of mosaic Down syndrome cases, the zygote has 46 chromosomes. Nondisjunction occurs during mitotic cell division and results in some cells or tissues having trisomy 21 and others not (Figure 4.3). By comparison, nondisjunction during meiosis followed by nondisjunction in some cells during mitosis after fertilization results in some cells losing the extra chromosome. Normal disjunction during meiosis followed by nondisjunction during mitosis results in the addition of an extra chromosome to some cells.

Depending on how far along the embryo is in development, mosaicism may affect part of the cells of one tissue or all of the cells of a particular tissue. In cellular mosaicism, some cells of a particular tissue, such as blood cells, have trisomy 21 and some do not. Tissue mosaicism occurs when all of the cells of a particular tissue, such as the skin, have trisomy 21 and other tissues do not. Since all cells or tissues are not trisomic, mosaicism results in fewer characteristics of Down syndrome on average. However, this varies with the affected individual.

Translocation that involves two different chromosomes is similar to **crossing over**, except that genetic material is exchanged with a member of a different chromosome pair. The most common translocation that results in Down syndrome is the transfer to chromosome 14 of an extra copy of part or all of chromosome 21. Either parent of a child with translocation Down syndrome may be a carrier. A carrier for translocation Down syndrome has 45 chromosomes but has the normal amount of genetic material because one copy of chromosome 21 has translocated to chromosome 14. This is the only type of Down syndrome that is hereditary.

PRENATAL TESTING

Women at higher risk for having a baby with Down syndrome sometimes choose to have prenatal screening or diagnostic tests performed. Prenatal screening tests called **multiple marker tests** measure the levels of certain proteins in the mother's blood. About 70% to 80% of Down syndrome cases can be detected with these tests. However, false positives, which indicate the presence of Down syndrome when the condition is not actually present, occur at a rate of about 5%. The results of these tests are combined with the age of the fetus and its mother to calculate the estimated risk of Down syndrome. Ultrasound measurements may also be factored into the equation.

If the risk of Down syndrome is perceived to be high, diagnostic tests may be performed in which a chromosomal **karyotype**, or analysis of the shape, size, and number of chromosomes in the cells. Fetal cells obtained from the amniotic fluid, from fetal cells that will form part of the placenta, or from umbilical cord blood are grown in the laboratory to produce a larger sample. This sample is stained so that the chromosomes are visible under the microscope and evaluated for any chromosomal abnormalities. Although diagnostic tests are more accurate than the screening tests, the procedures used to obtain the samples increase the risk of miscarriage by 1% to 2%.

Prenatal screening sometimes relieves anxiety during pregnancy for higher-risk mothers or helps them prepare emotionally for the birth of a baby with Down syndrome. It also provides an opportunity to use nutritional regimens to reduce the symptoms of Down syndrome in the developing fetus. That said, there are also ethical concerns among some parents of children with Down syndrome, who fear that prenatal screening will result in the reduction of the number of babies born with Down syndrome—thereby creating a disadvantage for children who are born with the disease.

5

DNA TECHNOLOGY

What we know about DNA and genes is the result of years of painstaking work by molecular geneticists. A number of sophisticated techniques have been developed that made these discoveries possible. Among the more common techniques employed by molecular geneticists are gel electrophoresis, Southern blotting, the polymerase chain reaction, DNA sequencing, and DNA microarrays. These and other techniques have made it possible to determine the sequences of genes on all of the chromosomes, including chromosome 21. Animal studies and DNA technology are used in research undertaken to determine the contribution of the extra genetic material in trisomy 21 to the physical characteristics that contribute to health conditions often associated with Down syndrome.

GEL ELECTROPHORESIS

Developed in the 1930s, **gel electrophoresis** is a technique that separates by size fragments of DNA molecules that have been cut by particular enzymes. Samples containing DNA fragments, a fluorescent dye, and a color dye are placed in a series of small wells across one end of a special rectangular gel that has been poured and solidified atop

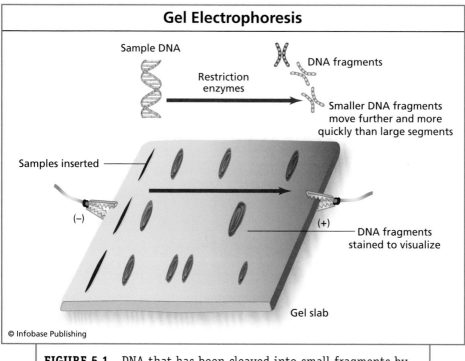

Gel Electrophoresis

Sample DNA

Restriction enzymes

DNA fragments

Smaller DNA fragments move further and more quickly than large segments

Samples inserted

(−)

(+)

DNA fragments stained to visualize

Gel slab

© Infobase Publishing

FIGURE 5.1 DNA that has been cleaved into small fragments by restriction enzymes is placed into wells in an electrophoresis gel at the end of the gel opposite the positive electrode. As an electrical current runs through the gel, the DNA fragments are segregated by size across the gel and form a band in which the number of fragments of various sizes can be counted.

a glass plate. The solution in which the DNA fragments are dissolved is denser than that with which the wells are filled, so that the protein molecules settle to the bottom. An electrical current is run through two electrodes at opposite ends of the gel apparatus. The negatively charged nucleotides are repelled by the negative electrode at the end of the apparatus near the wells and attracted by the positive electrode at the opposite end of the apparatus. Smaller fragments travel through the gel faster and farther than larger fragments. The color dye allows visual tracking of the movement of the fragments, and the fluorescent dye binds to the DNA. When the gel is viewed under an ultra-violet light, the samples have a banded appearance, with the larger fragments closer to the wells and the smaller fragments farther away.

SOUTHERN BLOT ANALYSIS

Developed by E.M. Southern, who published the procedure in 1975, the **Southern blot** is a method for extracting DNA fragments from a gel after electrophoresis. In this technique, DNA fragments are transferred to a nylon or nitrocellulose membrane and fixed to the membrane by ultraviolet radiation or drying. Either before or during the transfer, the gel is placed in an alkaline solution, such as a dilute solution of sodium hydroxide, so that the double-stranded DNA will separate into single strands. Further analysis of the DNA fragments can then be performed.

One analysis that is performed frequently involves exposing the blot to thousands of copies of a small radiolabeled single-stranded DNA fragment called a **probe.** The probe binds only to fragments of single-stranded DNA that have opposite (complementary) bases. After the membrane is washed of unbounded probe, X-ray film is placed over it and exposed. Darkened spots on the developed film show the position of DNA fragments with a sequence complementary to that of the probe. This film record is called an **autoradiogram**.

A similar blotting procedure can be done after separation of RNA molecules by gel electrophoresis and is called a northern blot. After the RNA has been transferred to a membrane, an RNA probe is used. Proteins can also be separated into polypeptides (chains of amino acids) by gel electrophoresis and transferred to a membrane. The blotting procedure in this case is called a western blot. A radiolabeled antibody is used as a probe for a particular polypeptide.

POLYMERASE CHAIN REACTION

Developed in the 1980s by American biochemist Kary B. Mullis, the **polymerase chain reaction (PCR)** revolutionized DNA technology and won this scientist the Nobel Prize in Chemistry in 1993. This technique is extremely sensitive and makes it possible to replicate a selected DNA sequence from a very small sample millions of times within a few hours. There are three steps to the procedure that are repeated over and over.

The first step is to heat a solution containing the double-stranded DNA sample to about 95°C for 15 to 30 seconds to break the hydrogen bonds between the paired bases so that the DNA molecules separate into single strands. Also in the solution are multiple copies of two primers, one complementary to a nucleotide sequence adjacent to one end of the target sequence on one strand and the other complementary to the same sequence on the other strand. Next, the solution is cooled to about 55°C for 30 seconds to allow primers to bind to their complementary sequences on the single-stranded DNA.

The solution is then heated to about 75°C, the optimum temperature for the Taq polymerase, for 1.5 minutes. After attaching the first nucleotide to one end of each primer, copies of this polymerase continue to add nucleotides until the reaction is stopped. Two new DNA fragments that contain the DNA target are produced that are much shorter than the original strands. The Taq polymerase was originally isolated from the bacterium *Thermus aquaticus*, which lives in the hot springs of Yellowstone National Park. It can survive the initial heat that unzips the sample DNA molecules and can remain in the PCR solution from the beginning to the end of the process.

Each time the three steps of this cycle are repeated, the number of copies of the target DNA sequence is doubled. It takes about 3 hours to make 1 million copies or 30 cycles to make 1 billion copies. This allows a large enough quantity of the target DNA sequence to be produced for further analysis, such as by gel electrophoresis.

DNA SEQUENCING

DNA sequencing involves determining the order of the nucleotide pairs in a gene or chromosome. All 3 billion base pairs of the human genome have now been sequenced. This was accomplished by The Human Genome Project, which began in 1990 and took 13 years to complete. The DNA sequencing technique most commonly used is the chain termination method developed in 1975 by British biochemist Frederick Sanger, who was awarded the Nobel Prize in Chemistry in 1980 for his accomplishment.

When nucleotides are added one at a time during DNA synthesis, the next nucleotide always attaches to the hydroxyl (OH-) group at the end of the nucleotide added before it. Since DNA polymerases will not add another nucleotide if this hydroxyl group is absent, the DNA chain will terminate right there. Synthetic nucleotides (called dideoxy-nucleotides), which do not have this terminal hydroxyl group, are used as chain-terminators in the Sanger procedure. The nucleotide chain to which a chain-terminator nucleotide attaches obviously always ends in the nucleotide to which the chain-terminator corresponds. Since this can happen anywhere on the DNA chain, the result is DNA fragments of many different lengths, all ending in the same nucleotide.

Newer technology and the PCR procedure have made modifications possible that have enhanced both the accuracy and speed of the process. Fluorescent (the most popular) and other nonradioactive methods are now used to label primers and the chain-terminator nucleotides. The fluorescent label for each of the four chain-terminator nucleotides (that correspond to the DNA nucleotides A, T, C, and G) emits a different light spectrum when excited. This makes it possible to put all four of them in one reaction mixture since they can be separated out by color later. Automated sequencing is now done in which the sample DNA is synthesized by primer extension as in PCR but with the fluorescent-labeled chain terminators added to the mixture along with the

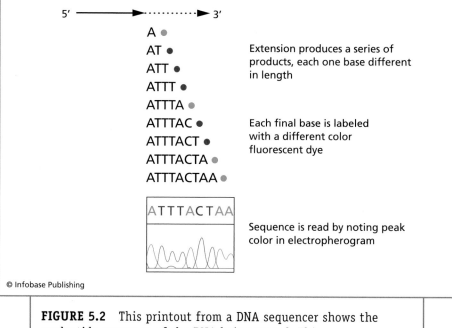

© Infobase Publishing

FIGURE 5.2   This printout from a DNA sequencer shows the nucleotide sequence of the DNA being tested. This sequence can then be used to determine which genes the DNA segment codes.

normal nucleotides. The fluorescent-labeled DNA fragments that are produced are then electrophoresed through either a very thin gel or through very thin (capillary) tubes made of glass. As the fragments separate and migrate, they pass a window through which the fluorescent labels are excited by a laser beam. A digital camera captures the light emissions and creates an image that is analyzed by a computer to produce a graph of the sequence produced by the four nucleotides, each of which is shown as a peak of a different color on the graph. Since much less heat is generated with the capillary tubes as opposed to the gel, that procedure is much faster. Increased recording accuracy is an advantage of both automated procedures.

DNA MICROARRAYS

One of the most recent innovations in DNA technology is the use of DNA microarrays. This technology has been particularly useful in studying the expression of genes in cells and tissues. Gene expression is the term used to refer to the transcription of a gene's DNA into mRNA, which in turn is translated into the gene's protein product. Although each cell has a complete set of chromosomes and a complete set of genes, each cell type expresses only a fraction of the full set of genes. For the cell to function properly, these particular genes must turn on and off at the right time in response to the right signals. Increases and decreases in expression of genes within the cell are tightly regulated.

About the size of a dime, the base of a microarray may be a glass slide, a nylon membrane, or a silicon chip. Onto this solid base, thousands of gene sequences are attached as microscopic spots in an orderly pattern so that each DNA sequence can be identified by its position on the

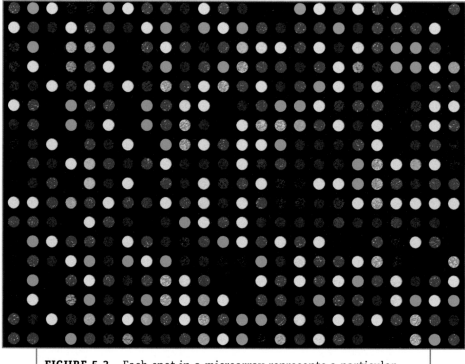

FIGURE 5.3 Each spot in a microarray represents a particular gene. The color and intensity of the fluorescence at each spot is an indicator of the quantity of that gene in the sample tissue.

microarray. The DNA sequences are single-stranded and may be DNA or oligonucleotides (short sequences of 5 to 50 nucleotides).

If a scientist wants to know which genes are expressed in a particular tissue, he or she extracts mRNA from that tissue and attaches a fluorescent label to the mRNA molecules, which are then incubated with the microarray. The mRNA molecules bind to the DNA sequences on the microarray to which they are complementary. Then the microarray is placed in a scanning device, where the fluorescent labels are excited by laser beams. A camera connected to a microscope creates a digital image that is analyzed by a computer. The computer analysis identifies the microarray spots that are "lit up" and the DNA sequence associated with each spot. It also calculates the relative intensity of the fluorescence at each spot to determine the ratios of the expressed genes in that tissue.

Sometimes a scientist will compare the gene expression of two different tissues, perhaps a normal (control) tissue and a diseased tissue to see whether they differ in the genes expressed. In this type of experiment, the mRNA from the two samples is labeled with fluorescent markers that fluoresce in two different colors. For example, the fluorescent color may be red for the disease sample and green for the control sample. The two samples are then mixed and incubated with the microarray. Analysis of the results indicate to which spots on the microarray the mRNA of each sample bound and with what intensity.

Either overexpression or underexpression of a gene can contribute to a disease state. Overexpression of a gene may be suspected if the fluorescence intensity for the mRNA of the diseased tissue is greater than that of the normal tissue at a particular spot on the microarray. Underexpression of a gene is indicated by a lower fluorescent intensity for the mRNA of the diseased tissue at a particular spot on the microarray. If the control sample mRNA binds to a spot on the microarray and the disease sample mRNA does not, that particular gene may be absent in the diseased tissue. This could point toward a genetic cause for the disease.

CHROMOSOME 21

In 2000, Masahira Hattori and colleagues reported that they had finished sequencing chromosome 21. They had sequenced 33,546,361 nucleotide pairs and found 225 genes on the long arm of chromosome 21. (Each chromosome is divided into two "arms" separated by the centromere. One arm is usually longer than the other and is called the long arm. Since chromosome 21 is very small, most of its genetic material is found in the long arm.) Subsequently, evidence accumulated that one region in particular seemed to be involved in some of the health problems associated with Down syndrome. This region was called the Down syndrome critical region.

Scientists are continuing to work to identify the specific genes on chromosome 21 that contribute to the developmental

RECOMBINANT DNA

Recombinant DNA technology involves the isolation and insertion of a gene into a **vector,** which is a self-replicating chromosome of a bacteria or virus. The vector that contains the gene is taken into a host cell, which may be a bacteria or a virus. This allows many copies of the gene to be replicated by the host cell progeny. Bacterial plasmids are the most commonly used vectors and are small, circular DNA molecules that occur in multiple copies in the bacterial cell in addition to the main chromosome.

Bacteria are unique in that they have enzymes called restriction endonucleases, which cut DNA on either side of specific nucleotide sequences that they recognize. There are dozens of restriction endonucleases, each of which recognizes a different nucleotide sequence. It is thought that restriction endonucleases are the bacterium's defense against bacteriophages, which are viruses that attack bacteria. Daniel Nathans and Hamilton Smith, who discovered restriction endonucleases in 1970, received the Nobel Prize in Physiology and Medicine in 1986 in recognition of this discovery. They shared the prize with Werner Arber, who was recognized for his pioneering research that made their discovery possible.

differences in Down syndrome. Several candidate genes have been identified that are overexpressed in Down syndrome or that appear to interact with other genes or transcription factors to produce certain characteristics typical of Down syndrome. The difficulty lies in the fact that there are so many interactions, not just among the genes on chromosome 21, but also with genes from other chromosomes. Slow progress is being made, however, in understanding how the extra genetic material on chromosome 21 induces changes in development

After DNA and plasmids have been isolated, a restriction endonuclease is added to both extractions. A particular sequence can be identified by running the DNA fragments through a gel and then applying a probe to a Southern blot of the gel. After the position of the desired fragment is identified on the gel, that band can be cut from the gel. Then the DNA fragments and the enzyme-digested plasmids are mixed together in a test tube so that the cut ends of the plasmids and the DNA fragments will bind. DNA ligase is added to the mixture to seal the ends together. Bacterial cells are then treated so that they will take up the plasmids.

When the plasmids replicate inside the bacterial cells, they also replicate the DNA fragment. Each plasmid vector that enters a bacterial cell replicates multiple times before the bacterium undergoes cell division. Eventually, a bacterial colony containing billions of copies of the DNA fragment is formed. Before the polymerase chain reaction was introduced, recombinant DNA technology was the only method available to obtain large quantities of a particular gene.

that produce the characteristics and health concerns of Down syndrome.

DNA FINGERPRINTING

Just as each individual has a unique set of physical fingerprints, the nucleotide sequence for the DNA of each individual is unique for that person. This genetic fingerprint has become very useful in the identification of accident victims, in paternity cases, and in identifying or ruling out crime suspects. Interestingly, it is the part of the DNA molecule for which a function has not yet been established that provides the clues for the DNA fingerprint.

There are several types of sequences in the DNA molecule that do not code for gene products. Two of these types are being used in combination with PCR technology for **DNA fingerprinting** (also called DNA profiling). One type is the variable number tandem repeat (VNTR), a DNA sequence composed of short repeated units of 15 to 100 nucleotides that occur in tandem (one behind the other). The number of repeats varies at different locations in the DNA molecule and also varies between individuals.

Another type of repetitive DNA that is highly individualized is composed of units of two to four nucleotides repeated in tandem. Therefore, they are called short tandem repeats (STRs). The number of repeats varies between individuals. STRs are more abundant and evenly distributed in DNA than variable number tandem repeats and are easier to work with in the laboratory. They may be used alone or in combination with variable number tandem repeats in DNA fingerprinting. To avoid false positives, a set of STRs and VNTRs that are less common are chosen. For example, four VNTRs are typically used and have a probability of producing

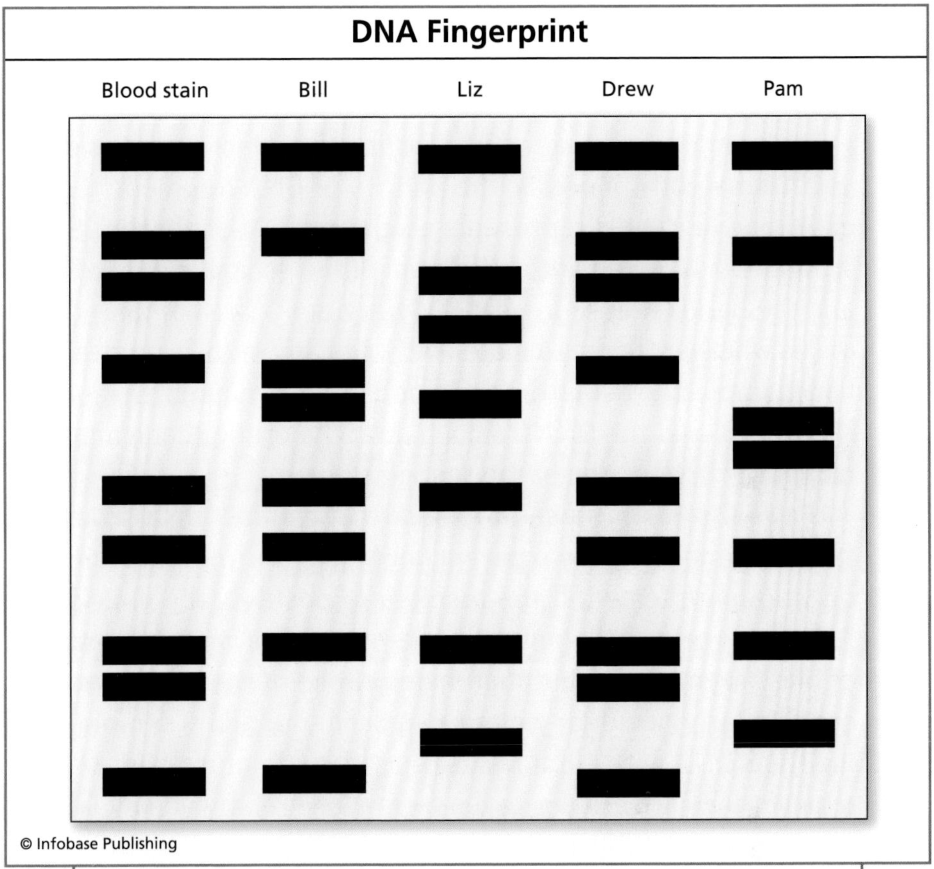

DNA Fingerprint

Blood stain	Bill	Liz	Drew	Pam

© Infobase Publishing

FIGURE 5.4 By comparing the sequence of DNA segments for each individual with that of the DNA sample, a blood stain can be matched with the appropriate person. In this illustration, the bands for Drew's DNA match those obtained from the blood stain.

a false positive of 1 in 1 million. A set of 13 STRs is typically used and has a probability of yielding a false positive of 1 in 1 trillion.

A very small sample of DNA can be used for DNA fingerprinting. A dried bloodstain or a hair from a crime scene is sufficient for forensic (crime-related) testing, for example. DNA extracted from one or more samples from the crime scene is reproduced in quantity by the PCR technique. DNA samples are also obtained from the victim and from suspects and are prepared in the same way. Then the individual samples are loaded into wells of an electrophoresis gel. After electrophoresis, the pattern of DNA fragments in each lane of the gel represents a separate DNA fingerprint. A Southern blot and autoradiogram of the gel are prepared, and the bands that represent DNA fragments are compared to see whether there is a match between any of the samples. For example, the DNA from the bloodstain may match that of the victim, and the DNA from a hair at the crime scene may match the DNA of one of the suspects.

Paternity testing uses a similar procedure. DNA from the child and the known parent, as well as the individual in question, are tested. If the results are positive, the child's DNA fingerprint will contain some bands that match those of one parent and some that match those of the other parent. Similarly, accident victims can be identified by comparing their DNA with samples such as strands of hair left on a hairbrush. Or samples taken from close relatives may be compared to establish identity.

6

HEALTH ISSUES IN DOWN SYNDROME

Differences in development resulting from the extra chromosome 21 genetic material contribute to a number of health problems that occur in a higher percentage of individuals with Down syndrome than in the general population. The presence and the severity of each of these conditions, however, vary with the individual. Advances in the treatment of these medical conditions have made it possible for individuals with Down syndrome to live longer and healthier lives.

HEART DEFECTS

About 40% to 50% of babies born with Down syndrome have heart defects, usually defects in the valves of the heart or in the walls between the chambers of the heart. The heart has four chambers, which are separated by muscular walls. The muscular wall that separates the left side of the heart from the right side of the heart is called the septum. There are two upper chambers called atria and two lower chambers called ventricles. Flaps of muscle called valves open and close the openings between the atria and the ventricles.

Under normal circumstances, oxygen-depleted blood from the body flows into the right atrium and then into the

Endocardial Cushion Defect

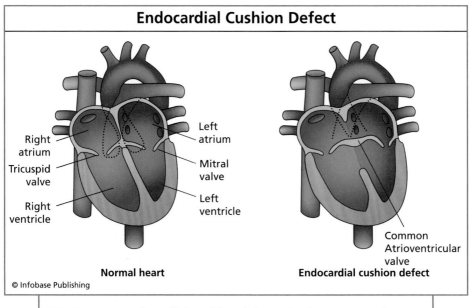

Normal heart

Endocardial cushion defect

© Infobase Publishing

FIGURE 6.1 Endocardial cushion defect, also known as atrioventricular septal defect, is a large hole in the center of the septum that involves both the atria and the ventricles. In complete atrioventricular septal defect, one large valve is present instead of the usual two. Both valves may be present in less severe forms of the defect.

right ventricle, from which it is pumped to the lungs, where it is replenished with oxygen. Oxygenated blood from the lungs then enters the left atrium, flows into the left ventricle, and is pumped out to the body. The oxygen-depleted blood on the right side of the heart does not mix with the oxygenated blood on the left side of the heart.

If there is a hole in either the wall between the atria or the wall between the ventricles, oxygen-depleted blood will mix with oxygenated blood. This can lead to the development of pulmonary hypertension, heart failure, or infections of the heart muscle. An opening between the two atria is called an **atrial septal defect** (ASD), and an opening between the two ventricles is called a **ventricular septal defect** (VSD). **Endocardial cushion defect,** also known as **atrioventricular septal defect** (AVSD), is a large hole in the center of the septum that involves both the atria and the ventricles.

The Atlanta Down Syndrome Project studied 227 infants diagnosed with Down syndrome over a 6.5-year period and found that 44% of these babies had heart defects. Of these, 45% were AVSD, and 35% were ventricular septal defects. Other defects were present in smaller percentages and sometimes in combination with either of the two more common defects.

Patent Ductus Arteriosus

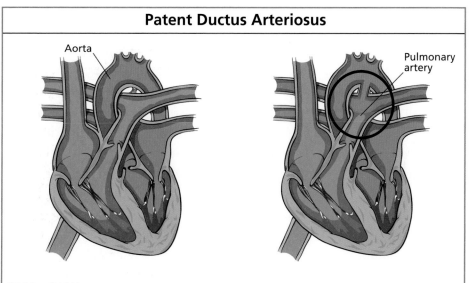

© Infobase Publishing

FIGURE 6.2   Another type of heart defect found with Down syndrome is patent ductus arteriosus. Before birth, a blood vessel called the patent arteriosus connects the aorta and the pulmonary artery so that blood does not go the lungs, which are not yet functioning. This connection normally closes within 24 hours after birth, but if it does not, blood will flow from the aorta through the pulmonary artery to the left side of the heart and then the lungs.

Before the advent of modern surgical techniques, heart defects resulted in early death for many babies with Down syndrome. This has been reduced significantly by early detection and correction. Echocardiography (ultrasound of the heart) is a reliable method of detecting septal and valve defects.

AVSD has a 5% survival rate to age 5 without surgery. Corrective surgery increases the survival rate to almost 70%. Children who have this surgery after age one are twice as likely not to survive the surgery. Because congenital heart defects are so common in infants with Down syndrome, it is recommended that they be monitored for heart problems with clinical examination and electrocardiography from shortly after birth until they reach adulthood.

Since 65% of AVSDs are found in individuals with Down syndrome, it is believed that an extra copy of one or more genes on chromosome 21 make these individuals more susceptible to the defect during development. Using Southern blot analysis, J.R. Korenberg's research team identified a region on chromosome 21 that was thought likely to contain genes related to congenital heart defects. A study by G.M. Barlow and colleagues narrowed this region to the gene for Down syndrome cell adhesion molecule (DSCAM) and proposed the DSCAM gene as a candidate gene for susceptibility to congenital heart disease in Down syndrome. **Cell adhesion molecules** (CAMs) are transmembrane (membrane-spanning) proteins that connect cells to each other or to the extracellular matrix, a complex mixture of proteins, carbohydrates, and other substances that surround the cells. Among other functions, CAMs are important in helping organs to form during embryonic development.

Complete AVSDs are 2,000 times more common in babies with Down syndrome than in the general population. Geneticist Cheryl Maslen and her research team at the Oregon Health

Sciences University have identified a mutation in the CRELD1 gene on chromosome 3 as a candidate for causing susceptibility to AVSD. The cell surface protein that CRELD1 encodes is thought to be a CAM, which gives it the potential of influencing embryonic development. In the general population, mutations in six to eight different genes are required to produce a heart defect. Maslen believes that trisomy 21 lowers this susceptibility threshold so that fewer additional mutations are required to produce in AVSD in a baby with Down syndrome.

GASTROINTESTINAL PROBLEMS

Children with Down syndrome experience problems with their digestive tract at a rate that is much higher than that of other children. Some of these problems, such as blockage of the digestive tract, can be life-threatening and may require emergency surgery. Blockage, or atresia, of the esophagus or the duodenum can cause starvation if not corrected. (The esophagus is the tube that carries food from the mouth to the stomach. The duodenum is the first part of the small intestine as it leaves the stomach.) Atresia is usually due to a failure of the structure to develop properly. Stenosis, in which narrowing occurs and slows the passage of food, can also occur.

Atresia of the anus occurs when the anal opening does not develop. This condition prevents solid waste from being eliminated from the intestinal tract and must be corrected surgically. Anal stenosis will allow waste products to pass, but will cause constipation.

Gastroesophageal reflux is also more common in individuals with Down syndrome. During gastroesophageal reflux, food reenters the esophagus from the stomach. This can cause vomiting and irritation of the esophagus. Reflux in Down syndrome is partially due to **hypotonia** (low muscle tone) in the esophageal sphincter, a circular muscle that surrounds the junction of the esophagus and stomach. This sphincter is usually closed except when food is passing through the esophagus. If medications or a change in diet do not help, surgery may be necessary to tighten the area where the esophagus and stomach join.

Celiac disease is an autoimmune disease that occurs in 5% to 12% of individuals with Down syndrome. It develops as an allergic response to gluten, a protein found in certain cereal grains such as wheat. Normally, the lining of the small intestine is folded into many villi, through which digested food is absorbed. After exposure to gluten, an immunologic response causes the villi to shrink, flattening the small intestine lining. The resulting problems with food absorption usually cause vomiting and/or diarrhea and can slow growth. A gluten-free diet, which eliminates wheat, rye, and barley, is the remedy. Oats are usually eliminated initially from the diet also because they can contain gluten from other grains that are processed by the same mill. It takes about 2 weeks for the gluten-free diet to work, but these grains must be kept out of the diet indefinitely. If the diet is not changed and the problems with food absorption continue, osteoporosis, anemia, and nerve damage can result.

About 2% of children with Down syndrome are born with Hirschsprung's disease, in which nerve cells are missing in the wall of the last part of the large intestine. As a result, that portion of the large intestine cannot produce the contractions necessary to move the waste material to the anus. Symptoms include vomiting, poor weight gain, a swollen abdomen, and chronic constipation. This problem is usually corrected by removing the section of intestine that is affected and joining the rest of the large intestine back together.

RESPIRATORY PROBLEMS

Individuals with Down syndrome have 12 times as many respiratory infections as other people. The death rate from respiratory infections is also higher in Down syndrome. Before the development of modern medical treatments, it was a significant cause of death among individuals with Down syndrome, especially children. Respiratory infections can be caused by viruses or bacteria. Colds, bronchitis, and pneumonia are examples of respiratory infections that affect the nasal passages, bronchial tubes, and lungs, respectively. A weak cough due to low muscle tone, fluid buildup in the lungs from congenital heart problems, regurgitation of stomach contents into the lungs, and immune system problems may contribute to the higher rate of respiratory infections in children with Down syndrome.

VISION PROBLEMS

Vision problems are common in individuals with Down syndrome. **Strabismus,** in which one or both eyes either turns in or out, occurs in 43% of children with Down syndrome. It is caused by abnormal or incomplete development of the centers in the brain that control the coordination of eye movements. This condition may require an eye patch, special glasses, or surgery. Vision therapy may also be of benefit and should be considered before surgery. If strabismus is not corrected, some vision may be lost in the crossed eye, creating partial blindness, a condition called **amblyopia** or "lazy eye."

Myopia, or nearsightedness, is found in 30% of individuals with Down syndrome. In this condition, the eyeball is too short, causing the light to focus on an imaginary point behind the retina. Distant objects appear blurred, whereas objects that are close are seen normally. Hypermetropia, or farsightedness, is found in 70% of individuals with Down syndrome. The eyeball is too long in this condition, and objects that are close focus in front of the retina. Far vision is normal, but close objects appear blurred. Either condition may affect only one eye, which makes the problem less likely to be noticed. Untreated, this can also result in amblyopia. It is recommended that regular eye exams start at age 6 months. Treatment for both conditions consists of corrective lenses (glasses).

Other eye problems that are more common in individuals with Down syndrome are cataracts, nystagumus, astigmatism, and blepharitis. Cataracts, found in 50% of individuals with Down syndrome, are caused by a clouding of the lens and are usually treated by surgical removal of the lens. The lens is the structure that focuses light rays on the retina. Nerve cells in the retina are stimulated by the various wavelengths of light and relay visual information to the brain, where it is interpreted. When the lens is clouded, light cannot pass through as well, and vision is blurred.

Nystagmus, found in 22% of individuals with Down syndrome, is a condition in which the eyes make uncontrollable jerky motions and can be caused by problems with the brain centers that control eye movement or by inner ear problems. There is evidence that deficiencies in magnesium and/or thiamine (Vitamin B2) may be contributing factors. Nystagmus often is seen with head injury, stroke, brain tumors, and multiple sclerosis. Each of these conditions can cause damage to the brain centers that control eye movements.

Blepharitis, found in 46% of individuals with Down syndrome, is an inflammation of the eyelids and can be treated with regular cleansing of the eyelids, lubricating drops, and topical antibiotics, as necessary, for infection. Astigmatism, found in 25% of individuals with Down syndrome, is caused by irregularities in the shape of the cornea and results in blurring of vision. The cornea, which covers the front of the eye, is a transparent protective membrane that lets light rays through and helps focus them through its curvature. Corrective lenses are usually used for astigmatism.

HEARING PROBLEMS

Anatomical differences that result from trisomy 21 contribute to the large percentage of hearing difficulties found in individuals with Down syndrome. Approximately 53% of children with Down syndrome have small ear canals. This makes it more difficult to examine the ears for wax buildup and infection. The middle ear is smaller than normal, as well. This contributes to the presence of chronic **otitis media** (ear infections) in 40% to 60% of children with Down syndrome. The shallow nasal bridge found in 61% of individuals with Down syndrome also contributes. Collapse or blockage of the Eustachian tube, which leads from the ear to the throat, causes fluid to build up in the middle ear and increases the risk of middle ear infection. In children with Down syndrome, the Eustachian tubes are often smaller than normal and have lowered muscle tone.

Problems with fluid buildup in the middle ear occur in about 60% of individuals with Down syndrome. This fluid buildup interferes with hearing and can cause permanent hearing loss if it remains for a long period of time. Estimates of hearing loss in people with Down syndrome range from 60% to 80%. Hearing loss in children can contribute to language and speech difficulties as well as auditory attention. Monitoring for fluid buildup and infections of the middle ear should begin before the age of 6 months and should continue into adulthood. Hearing aids may be an option to consider.

HYPOTHYROIDISM

Problems with the thyroid gland are common in individuals with Down syndrome. Weighing less than one ounce, the thyroid gland is actually one of the largest endocrine glands. Thyroid hormones help regulate the synthesis of growth factors and many hormones. They also affect all metabolic pathways. Thyroid hormones are crucial for proper brain development during pregnancy. They are also important in normal growth. Because they are composed of the amino acid tyrosine, to which iodine molecules have been attached, adequate iodine in the diet is essential for their production. Another hormone produced by the thyroid gland is calcitonin, which regulates the levels and metabolism of calcium.

The hormones tri-iodothyronine (T3) and tetra-iodothyronine (T4) are produced by the thyroid gland in a ratio of 1:14. T4 is secreted by the thyroid gland in response to TSH. The active form, T3, is primarily formed in the kidney, liver, and spleen by removal of one iodine molecule from T4. Selenium deficiency reduces the activity of the enzyme which converts T4 to T3. Receptors for T3 are located in the nucleus of each cell, and once T3 binds to its receptor, the hormone-receptor complex binds to thyroid-responsive elements (TREs) found in promoter regions of genes involved in growth and maturation.

Hypothyroidism refers to underactivity of the thyroid gland that results in the production of fewer thyroid hormones than normal. Hyperthyroidism is overactivity of the thyroid gland that results in higher levels of thyroid hormones than normal. When circulating blood levels of thyroid hormones are low, the pituitary increases its production of **thyroid-stimulating hormone** (TSH). An

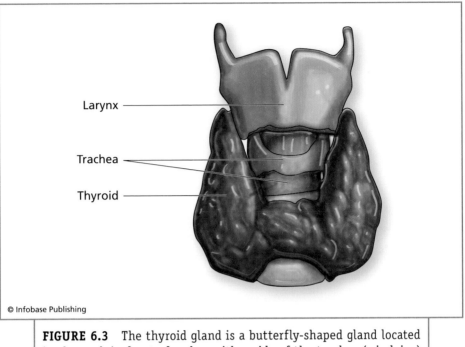

Larynx

Trachea

Thyroid

© Infobase Publishing

FIGURE 6.3 The thyroid gland is a butterfly-shaped gland located in the neck in front of and on either side of the trachea (windpipe) and below the larynx (voicebox).

elevated level of TSH is commonly considered an indicator for hypothyroidism. However, low levels of thyroid hormones can occur when TSH levels are within what is considered the normal range. Subclinical hypothyroidism may be indicated if TSH is elevated but the thyroid hormones are normal.

Based on current guidelines for levels of thyroid hormones that are considered within the normal range, hypothyroidism is found in 20% to 50% of individuals with Down syndrome, whereas hyperthyroidism is reported in about 2.5%. Thyroid autoantibodies (antibodies to thyroid hormones) are found in 29% to 40% of individuals with Down syndrome. Not usually seen before age 8, thyroid autoantibodies become more abundant with age. They may contribute to thyroid problems as the individual with Down syndrome ages.

However, symptoms of hypothyroidism may be present when laboratory tests are in the normal range. This is particularly important for children with Down syndrome, because hypothyroidism and Down syndrome share some of the same symptoms. In infants, these symptoms include a swollen tongue, a puffy face, low muscle tone, a large fontanelle ("soft spot"), herniated belly button, cold extremities, lethargy, mental retardation, little or no growth, low body temperature, thinning hair, orange skin, a hoarse cry, poor feeding, and persistent constipation. Having observed some of these symptoms in their children with Down syndrome despite "normal" laboratory tests, some parents see significant improvement in these symptoms after physicians administer thyroid hormone.

It is believed that many of the developmental and other health problems in Down syndrome may be related to hypothyroidism. Therefore, levels of the thyroid hormones, as well as TSH, should be tested at birth, at age 6 months and one year, and yearly thereafter through adulthood. If rapid weight gain, lethargy, sluggishness, decreased mental function, or other symptoms typical of hypothyroidism are noticed, the tests should be done more frequently. It has also been proposed that treatment with thyroxine (T4) beginning soon after birth may positively affect the growth and development of children with Down syndrome. T4 is used more often than T3 because it lasts longer in the body and can be administered once a day, whereas T3 must be administered in several doses per day. Sometimes T4 and T3 are combined for individuals who do not respond to T4 alone.

Supplementation with zinc may be beneficial to individuals with Down syndrome. Low zinc levels are associated with higher levels of TSH, and zinc supplementation has been shown to bring the TSH levels back to normal. Italian scientist Ines Bucci and colleagues found that zinc sulfate reduced TSH levels in hypothyroid patients with Down syndrome by 34% and improved thyroid function. Giorgio Napolitano and his colleagues reported that zinc sulfate increased growth in children with Down syndrome. Supplementation with zinc increases insulin-like growth factor type 1 (IGF-1), a zinc-containing growth factor that is deficient in children with Down syndrome after age 1.

LEUKEMIA

Individuals with Down syndrome are 10 to 30 times more likely to develop leukemia, a type of cancer caused by the production of abnormal white blood cells by the bone marrow. These abnormal cells eventually crowd out normal white and red blood cells. There are two main types of leukemia: acute and chronic. Acute leukemias develop slowly, and the patient's condition worsens more slowly. Chronic leukemias develop rapidly, and the patient's symptoms worsen quickly.

About 10% of babies born with Down syndrome develop a transient leukemia that usually goes away by 3 months of age. However, about 20% to 30% of those with this transient condition go on to develop acute leukemia. Babies who do not have Down syndrome rarely have the transient form of leukemia. This higher risk of leukemia is in contrast to the risk of other types of cancer in individuals with Down syndrome. The incidence of most types of solid tumors is much smaller than in the general population.

Overexpression of genes that inhibit tumor formation by one or more mechanisms may be a positive effect of some of the extra genetic material on chromosome 21.

Individuals who have Down syndrome are more sensitive to the toxicity of chemotherapy agents, especially methotrexate. This is because their white blood cells are more sensitive to mutagens and have poor DNA repair. This may be due in part to overexpression of three enzymes involved in the synthesis of the **purine** bases (adenine and guanine) that are located on chromosome 21. Supplementation with folic acid may lessen this toxicity to some extent.

IMMUNOLOGICAL PROBLEMS

Immune system function is diminished in Down syndrome. The immune system protects the body from disease by recognizing and attacking disease organisms. It includes the white blood cells and lymphoid organs such as the lymph nodes, spleen, bone marrow, thymus, and tonsils. Individuals with Down syndrome have a higher rate of respiratory and other infections as well as a higher risk of leukemia. Modern medical treatments have reduced the mortality associated with these illnesses. Death from pneumonia was 124 times higher in the Down syndrome population than for other individuals for the period from 1949 to 1959. This fell to a rate that was 62 times higher than the general population from 1960 to 1971. Death rates for other infections fell from 52 times to 12 times that of the general population during the same time frame.

Abnormalities in cells of the immune system and their products have been reported to be associated with Down syndrome. Lower antibody levels and cytokine production have been found in some studies. Antibodies, which are produced by certain white blood cells, either neutralize microorganisms directly or tag them for attack by other immune cells. Cytokines are the chemical messengers used by cells of the immune system (white blood cells) to communicate with each other and with other bodily systems, such as the nervous system and the endocrine system. The numbers of different types of immune cells and their responses to invading pathogens is also reduced.

Some of these abnormalities may be due to the overexpression of the gene for **superoxide dismutase,** which is found on chromosome 21. Superoxide dismutase is an enzyme that neutralizes superoxide radicals. A superoxide radical is basically an oxygen molecule with an extra electron that makes it more reactive. One of the byproducts of the neutralization of this free radical by superoxide dismutase is hydrogen peroxide. If produced in increased quantities, hydrogen peroxide could itself cause damage to cellular structures.

An excess of hydrogen peroxide may cause an increase in the enzyme glutathione peroxidase, which is required to break it down. This is turn produces an increased requirement for selenium, which is a necessary cofactor for this enzyme. Plasma levels of selenium have been found to be lower than normal in people with Down syndrome. Zinc, a cofactor for superoxide dismutase, is also lower than normal in plasma of individuals with Down syndrome. The overactivity of superoxide dismutase and glutathione peroxidase may reduce the body's store of these essential trace minerals. M. Abdalla and S. Samman found that zinc supplementation reduced superoxide dismutase in females who did not have Down syndrome. Maintaining an optimal level of zinc may be important to reduce the effects of overproduction of superoxide dismutase and hydrogen peroxide due to the overexpression of the SOD1 gene.

The gene for the interferon receptor is also found on chromosome 21. Interferon is a cytokine that is important in the body's defense against viruses. It can also slow the rate of growth of cancer cells. Dr. Leonard Maroun believes that the effect of too much interferon is harmful and may actually produce some of the developmental differences seen in Down syndrome. It is thought that interferon levels in people with Down syndrome are normal, but that overexpression of the interferon receptor makes them overly sensitive to the effects of interferon.

Using a mouse model of Down syndrome, which has an extra copy of chromosome 16 (the mouse equivalent of chromosome 21), Maroun has shown that treating the mother rat with anti-interferon antibodies results in fewer abnormalities in her offspring. Maroun has also noted that many of the side effects of interferon therapy for other conditions match some of the developmental differences seen in Down syndrome. Among these side effects are memory loss, neurotoxicity, cardiotoxicity, autoimmune disease, deafness, and growth retardation. Work is under way to develop an interferon antagonist for use in humans.

Another gene involved in immune function that is found on chromosome 21 is the gene for lymphocyte function associated antigen-1 (LFA-1). Abnormalities in the maturation of immune cells in the thymus gland may be caused by the overexpression of this protein. The lower plasma levels of zinc and selenium found in individuals with Down syndrome can also contribute to a weakened immune system. Supplementation with these minerals appears to strengthen immune function.

MUSCULOSKELETAL PROBLEMS

A number of problems that affect the muscular and skeletal systems are more common in individuals with Down syndrome. Loose joints and low muscle tone are among the most common of these. Joint laxity (loose joints) affects about 44% of children between ages 6 and 10 with Down syndrome, with the percentage decreasing as the children grow older. This condition is due to looseness of the ligaments that attach muscles to bone and bones to each other. The ligaments are loose because the collagen protein of which they are made is abnormal, due to the effects of overexpression of collagen (type VI), the gene for which is found on chromosome 21. Hypotonia (low muscle tone) is one of the diagnostic features of Down syndrome used for a newborn. Most of the joint-related problems in Down syndrome are caused by a combination of joint laxity and hypotonia.

Atlanto-axial instability is found in 10% to 20% of children with Down syndrome. Flexible joints and low muscle tone seem to be the underlying factors in this condition, which involves looseness in the first two vertebrae in the neck. The first vertebra in the neck is the atlas, the second one is the axis, and the joint between them is the atlanto-axial joint. This joint allows the head to rotate and the neck to bend forward and backward, and to a small extent, laterally. If the space between them becomes too large, usually more than 5 mm, they can slip, causing atlanto-axial **subluxation**. A subluxation is a partial dislocation. This can cause damage to the spinal cord, with accompanying neurological problems. Subluxation occurs in about 1% to 2% of children with Down syndrome. Dislocation of the atlanto-axial joint can also occur. A dislocation is a misalignment or displacement of the bones of a joint and also involves damage to the associated ligaments.

Because of the higher risk of neck problems in children with Down syndrome, it is recommended that they have a neck X-ray at age 2 and every 2 years thereafter until they reach adulthood. If a measurement of 4.5 mm or greater between the atlas and axis joints is found, restriction on sports that put pressure on the neck as it bends is advised. Restriction from all strenuous activities is recommended if a subluxation or dislocation occurs. Sometimes surgery is performed to correct a subluxation, especially if there are neurological symptoms.

Scoliosis, or abnormal curvature of the spine, is seen more often in people with Down syndrome. It is thought to have affected up to half of individuals with Down syndrome who were institutionalized. Hip abnormalities are found in 5% to 8% of individuals with Down syndrome. Most common among these is hip subluxation due to low muscle tone combined with laxity of the ligaments that hold the femur (thigh bone) in its socket in the pelvic bone. Hip subluxation usually develops between ages 3 and 13 in susceptible children with Down syndrome.

Patellar (kneecap) instability is found in almost 20% of individuals with Down syndrome. Subluxation is present in most cases of patellar instability, but dislocation can also occur. With subluxation, the kneecap can be moved farther to the side than normal. If the kneecap is dislocated, it is moved completely out of position and may be difficult to put back in place. Either condition causes a change in gait and in the knee's range of motion. If left untreated, instability of the kneecap will worsen over time.

Pes planus, or flat feet, is found in most people with Down syndrome. Heavy calluses form on the feet, and the toes point outward during walking. It is common in individuals with Down syndrome for the joint behind the big toe to protrude outward. This condition can develop into painful bunions and makes it difficult to find shoes that fit. Joint problems in general are more common in Down syndrome. Some of them may be due to hypermobility of the joints because of looseness of the ligaments.

Umbilical hernias are found in 90% of children with Down syndrome. In this condition, the navel protrudes because the umbilical ring, a muscle surrounding the navel, fails to close. Part of the abdominal lining or organs may protrude through the opening. The size of the hernia can range in diameter from less than 1 mm to more than 5 mm. Those that are less than 1 mm in diameter usually close on their own within three to four years. Larger hernias that do not close may require surgery.

SKIN PROBLEMS

A number of dermatological (skin) problems are common with Down syndrome. During infancy, the skin is soft and velvety. Cutis marmorata, in which the skin has a bluish mottled appearance, is seen in about 8% to 13% of infants with Down syndrome. This is a common condition in newborns in the general population, but its duration is several months longer with Down syndrome.

By late childhood, the skin becomes dry and rough in 70% of children with Down syndrome. This condition is called xerosis. Cracks and red, scaly skin at the mouth corners, a condition called chelitis, is present in about 6%. About 50% of individuals with Down syndrome have atopic dermatitis, in which red, itchy, scaly skin is present, primarily behind the ears and knees, on the cheeks, and in the creases of the elbow. Very thick skin on the soles of the feet and on the palms is called palmoplantar hyperkeratosis. This condition is not present before age 5 months, but there is an incidence of 75% in children with Down syndrome age 5 years and over.

A variety of skin infections are more common in Down syndrome. Folliculitis is an infection or inflammation of the hair follicles. It may be caused by either bacteria or fungi and looks like yellowish pustules or red bumps. A microscopic mite causes the skin condition called scabies. Symptoms, which include an itchy rash of small red dots, are worse in people with Down syndrome.

Alopecia areata, in which patches of hair in the scalp fall out, is seen in 5% to 9% of individuals with Down syndrome. It is thought to be an autoimmune disease that destroys hair follicles in the affected areas. At least some of the hair grows back in most people, but it can become a chronic condition without regrowth. A candidate gene called MX1 on chromosome 21 has been identified for this condition. If the entire scalp is affected, the condition is called alopecia totalis. Loss of hair over the entire body is called alopecia universalis and is found in only a very small percentage of individuals.

Vitiligo is the loss of pigmentation in well-defined areas of skin that can occur anywhere on the body. It is thought to be due to an autoimmune process in which melanocytes (pigment-producing skin cells) are destroyed. Percentages are not that high in Down syndrome but are higher than in the general population. Acanthosis nigrans occurs in about 50% of individuals with Down syndrome. Symptoms include an increase in pigment, with the affected area of skin being scaly and elevated. It usually occurs on the hands, on the back of the neck, or in the groin area. Premature wrinkling of the skin also occurs in Down syndrome.

7

DOWN SYNDROME
AND THE BRAIN

The exceptional achievements of young people with Down syndrome such as actor/musician Chris Burke, actress Ruth Cromer, author Mitchell Levitz, and actor Jason Kingsley demonstrate the potential of children with this disorder. This is particularly noteworthy because children with Down syndrome have not always been given the same opportunities to learn and achieve that other children usually receive.

From the 1920s to the 1960s, individuals with cognitive disabilities were often institutionalized—sent to live in a facility where they would be under supervision. During the 1960s and 1970s, however, a movement was started to protect the civil rights of people with disabilities. This movement resulted in the discharge of many disabled adults from institutions and a decline in the number of children accepted by them.

Legislation was created to protect the rights of children with disabilities and to ensure that they had access to the same education as their peers. Early legislation on this topic established the right of disabled children to Free Appropriate Public Education (FAPE). The first law was the Education for the Handicapped Act (EHA) of 1975. Amendments to EHA in 1986 extended FAPE to children ages 3 to

5 and established an Early Intervention Program (EIP) for children of ages 0 to 2. The 1990 EHA amendments renamed the act as the Individuals with Disabilities Education Act (IDEA) and established the right of disabled children to the Least Restrictive Environment (LRE), to permit inclusion in the regular classroom as much as possible. Additional provisions have been added by other amendments over the years. Each state has also passed legislation to address the educational needs of children with disabilities.

The struggles of parents to obtain a quality education for their children with Down syndrome led to slow progress toward the goal of obtaining an optimal education for every child, including those with disabilities. Many children with Down syndrome who have been given appropriate educational opportunities have far exceeded the low expectations once held for them by society. Treatment programs that address the metabolic differences induced by the extra genetic material, as well as other developmental differences, have also enabled many children with Down syndrome to achieve at previously unexpected levels.

IQ AND DOWN SYNDROME

The first intelligence test was developed by French psychologist Alfred Binet in 1905 with the sole purpose of identifying children with "inferior" intelligence so that they could be placed in special schools to address their special needs and to keep them from disrupting the learning of "normal" children. Binet warned that that his scale, strictly speaking, was not a measure of intelligence—that intelligence could not be defined by a single score, and that intelligence was not a fixed quantity that could not be improved.

However, despite Binet's warnings, his test became the foundation for a testing industry whose products were in

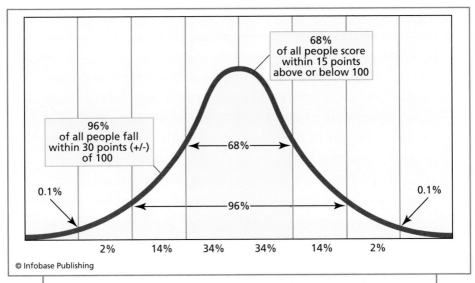

FIGURE 7.1   As proposed by Lewis Terman in 1916, an IQ score between 90 and 109 is considered to represent average intelligence. A score over 140 is considered genius or near genius. People with scores below 70 are considered "feeble-minded" or mentally retarded. However, the ability of the IQ test to accurately measure intelligence has been called into question.

mass use by the 1920s and became accepted by educators as accurate, scientifically sound measures of intellectual potential. The term IQ (for intelligence quotient) was introduced in 1912 by German psychologist William Stern and has been used to describe the score obtained by a variety of different tests.

For the first half of the twentieth century, most people with Down syndrome were considered to be severely retarded, functioning at a cognitive level significantly below average. Then, during the 1960s, the majority of people with Down syndrome were considered moderately to severely retarded, with up to 10% being considered mildly retarded. By the mid-1970s, a small number were classified in the normal range of cognitive development, with up to 30% to

50% being considered mildly retarded. There were many children with Down syndrome whose IQ scores were in the normal to above-average range by the 1990s. An IQ score of 140, an exceptionally high score, was reported for one child with Down syndrome. This rise in IQ scores may be a result of the effects of deinstitutionalization, as well as a change in the expectations of parents and teachers as they gradually pushed the upper limits set for their children by society. It also reflects the success of combined nutritional and developmental therapy programs that became available.

Many professionals believe that too much emphasis has been placed on the IQ score for estimating the cognitive capacity of children with disabilities, or for that matter, of children in general. Performance on these tests can be affected by physical disabilities, such as the high rate of visual and hearing impairment found in children with Down syndrome. Learning disabilities can also mask other talents and abilities.

Scientists such as Banesh Hoffman and Stephen Jay Gould have protested the ways in which the IQ tests have been used to define the quality of a person. A criticism raised by Canadian educational psychologist Linda Siegel is that IQ tests do not measure problem solving, critical thinking, logical reasoning, and adaptation, which are usually included in definitions of intelligence. Instead, memory skills, specific knowledge, expressive language, vocabulary, fine motor coordination, visual-spatial abilities, perceptual skills, and even speed are important for obtaining a high score. In Dr. Siegel's opinion, the IQ test measures what the child has already learned rather than what that child's potential capabilities are. She believes that the IQ test should not be administered to children with learning disabilities because they already have deficiencies in one or more of the component skills of IQ tests, such as fine motor, language, or memory difficulties. Their reasoning and problem-solving skills could very well be superior to a child who does not have these problems and scores higher on the test. By relying on IQ test scores, the true intelligence and potential of a child with a learning disability is likely to be underestimated.

It has also been erroneously stated that the IQ score of children with Down syndrome declines with age. If the average mental age of a group of children with Down syndrome is plotted across time, it will go upward more slowly than that of the general population, but it will go steadily upward. Because the IQ score is obtained by comparing a child's mental age with that of other children the same age, this slower increase in mental age has been misinterpreted as a decline in intelligence.

READING AND SPEECH DEVELOPMENT

One strategy that has been used successfully to encourage language production is teaching preschoolers with Down syndrome to read words from flash cards. Single words are used at first, then two-word phrases, then three-word phrases. Some of these children can learn to read single-word flash cards as early as age 2 and most of them by age 3 or 4. Learning to read at an early age enhances speech development as the words learned from the flash cards become part of the children's spoken language. British developmental psychologist Sue Buckley researched and developed this procedure after receiving a letter in 1980 from a father who had taught his daughter with Down syndrome to read from flash cards beginning at age 3. Learning to read while learning to speak has greatly improved the academic potential of many children with Down syndrome.

NEURONAL DEVELOPMENT

Scientists have attempted to find the underlying causes for the cognitive difficulties experienced by some individuals with Down syndrome. Studies of postmortem brains done in the 1980s concluded that neuronal development in fetuses with Down syndrome was normal, but that the dendritic trees did not increase in complexity as the children grew older. Dendrites are the nerve fibers that receive information from other neurons. Most neurons have dendrites with many branches that form what is called a dendritic tree. Brain development itself, including **myelination,** appears normal at the time of birth in infants with Down syndrome. **Myelin** is the fatty covering around some nerve fibers that provides an insulation that allows electrical messages to travel through the fibers faster. Relatively minor differences are found at birth. More noticeable differences seem to begin to emerge after the age of 2 months, with structures such as the hippocampus and cerebellum, which finish development after birth, being the most affected. This could very well be the result of metabolic and endocrine disturbances that went untreated.

Physician Joseph D. Pinter and colleagues used magnetic resonance imaging (MRI) to study the brain volumes of a group of 16 people with Down syndrome ages 5 to 23. They used a control group of 15 young people who did not have Down syndrome and were matched by age and gender to the people in the group that did have Down syndrome. Compared with the control group, the brain volumes of the children with Down syndrome in this study were 18% smaller overall. However, it is possible that some of this difference was due to difference overall in size, since children with Down syndrome tend to be significantly smaller than the general population.

After the MRI data were adjusted for the difference in overall volume, the researchers did find that the cerebellum was disproportionately smaller in the subjects with Down syndrome. This may account for the low muscle tone and speech difficulties seen with Down syndrome. Some cognitive functions may also be affected by smaller cerebellar volumes. However, the subcortical gray matter (neuronal tissue) and the parietal lobe gray matter were proportionately larger than in the control group. The parietal lobe is responsible for the integration of the senses, and this finding may account for the relative strength in visuospatial processing in individuals with Down syndrome. The temporal lobe was also relatively larger because of a larger volume of white matter (nerve tracts). There were no differences after adjustment in volume for the frontal and occipital lobes. The visual cortex is found in the occipital lobes, and the motor cortex—as well as the cortex responsible for the higher cognitive functions—are found in the frontal lobes.

Previous studies in older individuals noted similar differences in overall brain size and cerebellar volume. In addition, differences in volume of other structures such as the hippocampus had been noted. Mohammed Rachidi and colleagues at the Pasteur Institute in Paris believe that overexpression of the C21orf5 gene may be responsible for some of the anatomical changes seen in the brains of individuals with Down syndrome. This chromosome 21 gene is selectively expressed in the fetal hippocampus, cerebellum, and cerebrum, making it a candidate for contributing to difficulties with cognitive functions that are dependent on these brain structures. Rachidi's research team also found a similar distribution of another chromosome 21 gene, the transcription factor SIM2, which appears to be important in neurodevelopment. Rosa Ferrando-Miguel and colleagues at the University of Vienna in Austria found that the transcription factor BACH1 was overexpressed in fetal Down syndrome brain.

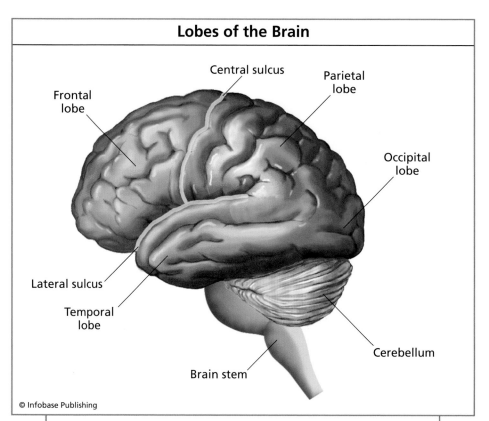

Lobes of the Brain

© Infobase Publishing

FIGURE 7.2 Based on function and location, the cerebral cortex is divided into four lobes. Visual information is received and processed by the visual cortex. Somatosensory information is received by the parietal lobe and integrated with information from the other senses. Auditory information is received and processed by the temporal lobe. Temporal lobe structures are also involved in emotion and learning and memory. Higher cognitive functions, such as planning and judgment, are performed by the frontal lobe. Motor cortex, which controls movement, is also found in the frontal lobe. The cerebellum is involved in movement coordination and posture as well as in motor skill learning.

Another chromosome 21 gene that has received a lot of attention is the MNB gene, which is expressed during embryonic development at about the same time that neuronal dendritic trees are developing. MNB kinase, the enzyme product of the MNB gene, is transported to the developing dendritic tree and may influence its development. Over-expression of this gene in mice has been found to cause delayed brain development, decreased motor-skill learning, and significant deficits in reference memory and spatial memory.

THYROID FUNCTION AND THE BRAIN

Cretinism, characterized by stunted growth and mental retardation, is the outcome of untreated hypothyroidism during infancy and childhood. This disorder is now preventable by early treatment of the underlying thyroid problems. In some cases, this is as simple as adding iodine to the diet. Given the similarities between some of the symptoms of hypothyroidism and characteristics once thought to be typical of Down syndrome, Miriam Kauk and others believe that physical and mental growth and development in children with Down syndrome can be improved by identifying and treating symptoms of hypothyroidism.

Hypothyroidism can negatively affect any of the many functions of the thyroid hormones in brain development and function. There are thyroid hormone receptors present in the brain by the tenth week of gestation. Thyroid hormones influence the transcription of genes that code for growth factors, neurotransmitters, and neuronal (nerve cell) structural elements. Proteins involved in the myelination of nerve fibers are also influenced by thyroid hormones. In addition, a deficiency of thyroid hormones reduces the number of dendritic spines in the auditory (hearing) cortex and in neurons in the visual cortex. Dendritic spines are thornlike projections on the branches of dendrites to which axons from other neurons connect. In rats whose thyroid gland has been removed, glucose use is profoundly reduced throughout the brain. Glucose is the only fuel that the brain uses for its activities, except in times of starvation, when ketones produced by protein breakdown are used as an alternative fuel.

Some of the symptoms that have been associated with hypothyroidism are memory impairment, ataxia (loss of balance and coordination), confusion, hallucinations, psychotic behavior, and delusions. Symptoms of hyperthyroidism include a fast heart rate, trembling, sweating, restlessness, and anxiety. This may progress to irritability, nervousness, and sleep disturbances. More severe cases exhibit paranoia, depression, and mania. Extreme cases may experience delirium, followed by stupor and coma. Dementia is seen with hypothyroidism in elderly patients. Hypothyroidism is also considered a risk factor for Alzheimer's disease.

During development as well as adulthood, thyroid hormones have a significant influence on the function of certain brain structures, especially the hippocampus, septal nuclei, cerebellum, and cerebral cortex. The cortex is the thin layer of nervous tissue that covers the cerebral cortex. Deep inside the cerebral hemispheres beneath the cortex are found the hippocampus and the septal nuclei, which work together in learning and memory as well as other functions. Perched atop the brainstem at the back of the brain is the cerebellum, which is involved in the coordination of movements. Thyroid hormone deficiency during the perinatal period (from 5 months before birth until 7 days after birth) adversely affects brain development, including the development of some of the neurotransmitter systems. Neurotransmitters are the chemical messengers released by neurons to communicate with other neurons. Delayed myelination and mental retardation are among the abnormalities caused by hypothyroidism during the perinatal period.

A close relationship has been found between the thyroid hormones and cholinergic neurons in certain septal nuclei and their pathways to the hippocampus. This relationship is evident from the perinatal period throughout adulthood. Nerve growth factor (NGF), which is important to cholinergic function, and the thyroid hormones appear to work together to enhance cholinergic activity. Their combined effects are greater than the sum of their separate effects, which is typical of a synergistic relationship, or synergism.

Cholinergic neurons produce the neurotransmitter acetylcholine. There is an important nerve pathway from cholinergic neurons in the basal forebrain to the hippocampus. The hippocampus is necessary for the formation of new memories about information and events. Both the hippocampus and the septal nuclei begin to deteriorate in the earlier stages of Alzheimer's disease. One of the hallmarks of Alzheimer's disease is a decline in memory functions. Loss of cholinergic neurons is typical of Alzheimer's disease and is thought to underlie some of the memory loss found in that disease.

MOTOR DEVELOPMENT

In the past, children with Down syndrome have typically taken longer to reach developmental milestones, such as sitting up, crawling, and walking, than have other children. Low muscle tone and joint laxity slow their motor development. Earlier developing motor skills are only slightly delayed. Rolling over may take place from 5 to 6.4 months and sitting alone by 8.5 to 11.7 months. Motor skills that usually develop later are more delayed in children with Down syndrome. Crawling occurs between 12.2 and 17.3 months, and walking occurs between 15 and 74 months. (A child who does not have Down syndrome typically walks before 18 months.) However, interventions now available for children with Down syndrome are reducing these delays.

LANGUAGE DEVELOPMENT

Language production tends to be delayed in children with Down syndrome. Babbling in infants seems normal. However, about 50% of children with Down syndrome show delays in language production by the time their mental age score reaches 24 months. Almost all children with Down syndrome show deficits by the time they reach a mental age of 36 months. Vocabulary skill deficits are found in only 50% of children with Down syndrome, but delays in learning grammar are found in most Down syndrome individuals by a mental age of 36 months.

Contributing factors to the delays seen in language production include hearing loss, a relative weakness in auditory verbal memory (remembering words that are said), hypotonia of muscles involved in speech production, a small mouth cavity that causes the tongue to protrude, swollen vocal cords, and developmental differences in facial muscles. The muscles that attach to the upper lip are fused in people with Down syndrome instead of separate as in the general population. An extra facial muscle reaching from the mouth corner to the back of the head is present in Down syndrome. These muscle differences limit lip movement and contribute to difficulties with speech production.

Children with Down syndrome vary in the rate at which language production develops. They say their first words anywhere from 9 months to 7 years of age, compared with 6 to 14 months in normally developing children. Two-word combinations or simple sentences are produced anywhere from 18 months to 11 years, as compared with 14 to 32 months in children without Down syndrome. Language production in adults with Down syndrome ranges anywhere from limited language to a high level of fluency. Interventions now available can make a difference in the language development of children with Down syndrome. Some young people with Down syndrome are even learning foreign languages.

Language comprehension is stronger than language production in children with Down syndrome. Word learning appears to be normal in early childhood. Syntax, the way in which words are organized into sentences, is more difficult for them. In other words, children with Down syndrome seem to understand more of what they hear than they can communicate verbally. They tend to use gestures more than other children to make up for this deficit. The difference in strength between language comprehension and language production appears at about a mental age of 18 months. According to Robin Chapman, who specializes in communication disorders, the development of speech comprehension skills in individuals with Down syndrome plateaus during adolescence, but speech expression (production) skills continue to improve. Language training and speech therapy can produce improvements in language skills, even into adulthood.

MEMORY

Individuals with Down syndrome have lower than normal scores on memory tests that require them to listen to and repeat a spoken series of numbers or words. These tests are supposed to measure verbal short-term memory, memory that is used to hold on to information long enough to use it in a task but does not store the information permanently. For information to be stored permanently, it must be transferred into long-term memory, where it may remain for a lifetime.

The average person can hold seven items of information in short-term memory. Individuals with Down syndrome usually cannot hold that many items in their auditory short-term memory, or short-term memory for words or other sounds. However, their visual short-term memory, or short-term memory for pictures or objects that they see, is consistent with their mental age. Individuals with Down syndrome also have more difficulties with spatial memory, or memory for locations. Spatial memory is one of the functions of the hippocampus, a brain structure that has been shown to be smaller in some individuals with Down syndrome.

Individuals with Down syndrome also have more difficulty with long-term memory tasks that involve recalling information or events. This type of memory is called explicit, or declarative, memory. It is easy to put into words and is available for conscious recall. The formation of explicit memories is heavily dependent on the hippocampus. However, individuals with Down syndrome perform consistent with their mental age on nondeclarative, or implicit, memory tasks. Implicit memory involves learning skills or rules that are not easily put into words and are not readily recalled consciously. The basal ganglia and the cerebellum, which is sometimes smaller in those with Down syndrome, are brain structures that are important in implicit memory.

SEIZURES

Seizure disorders occur more often in people with Down syndrome. Adult-onset epilepsy occurred in 36.8% of individuals with Down syndrome in one 12-year study. Seizures in infants occur 8 to 10 times more frequently than in the

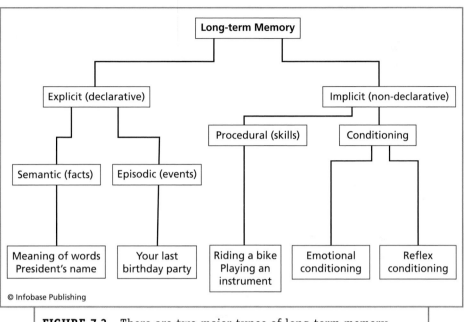

© Infobase Publishing

FIGURE 7.3   There are two major types of long-term memory—declarative (explicit), and nondeclarative (implicit). Explicit memory can be recalled consciously and includes memories of facts (semantic memory) and events (episodic memory). Implicit memory is more difficult to describe verbally and includes skill learning and memory of rules, such as the rules of grammar.

general population. Adults who have both Down syndrome and Alzheimer's disease have more seizures than adults with Alzheimer's disease alone.

Naturopath and nutritionist Robert J. Thiel, who is director of the Down Syndrome-Epilepsy Foundation and co-director of the Center for Natural Health Research, and organic chemist Steven W. Fowkes, who is head of the Cognitive Enhancement Research Institute (CERI), have pointed out a number of nutritional deficiencies that occur more often in individuals with Down syndrome as well as in people who have epilepsy. These deficiencies may be due to poor absorption, errors in metabolism, or,

in the case of people with epilepsy, the effects of anticon-
vulsant drugs. Vitamin deficiencies are more frequent in
these two groups than in the general population, including
deficiencies in vitamin A, thiamine (marginal with Down
syndrome), vitamin B6, folate, vitamin B12, vitamin C,
and vitamin D. Blood plasma levels of vitamin E are significantly lower in people with Down syndrome and more
so in those with dementia. Vitamin E has been shown in
a controlled study to reduce seizures in children with
epilepsy. Vitamins B6 and B12 have also been shown to
reduce seizures in epilepsy. Deficiencies in vitamin B6 or
vitamin B12 can actually trigger seizures.

Decreased levels of calcium within the cells and in the
hair have been found in individuals with Down syndrome.
Calcium deficiency may trigger seizures. Deficiency in copper is another cause of seizures. Although it is not implicated in epilepsy, iron levels may be low in children with
Down syndrome. Levels of magnesium, manganese, and
selenium have been found to be lower than normal more
frequently both in individuals with Down syndrome and
people with epilepsy. Either magnesium deficiency or selenium deficiency can trigger seizures. Several studies indicate that individuals with Down syndrome have lower than
normal levels of zinc in plasma. Zinc deficiency can also
trigger seizures.

Levels of the amino acids cysteine and phenylalanine are
high in individuals with Down syndrome, due to enzymatic
problems. Significant deficits in plasma serine have been
found in people with Down syndrome. Deficiency of serine
is associated with seizures. People with seizure disorders
have reduced levels of the amino acid tryptophan in the
plasma and cerebrospinal fluid, possibly due to hyperme-
tabolism of tryptophan. (Cerebrospinal fluid is the fluid
that surrounds the brain and spinal cord). It is thought that

tryptophan metabolism is abnormal in Down syndrome also. Muscle tone in infants with Down syndrome improved after tryptophan supplementation in one study.

ALZHEIMER'S DISEASE

Alzheimer's disease is a progressive neurodegenerative disease that occurs in about 11% of people over age 60. Memory loss is one of the primary symptoms of the disease. Gradual deterioration in other mental functions usually follows, and with an immune system weakened by the ravages of the disease, the Alzheimer's patient dies, usually from infections, within 1 to 20 years. When the brains of Alzheimer's patients are examined after death, two neuropathological changes are consistently found. One of these is the deposition of an abnormal form of beta-amyloid protein (Aß) in plaques outside of neurons. The other is the buildup inside neurons of tangles consisting of filaments of an abnormal form of tau protein.

Both beta-amyloid plaques and neurofibrillary tangles occur in normal aging but not in such quantity. It is thought that excessive levels of Aß inside neurons, rather than the Aß plaques outside them, is what causes neurodegeneration. An inflammatory response is triggered by excessive Aß. Microglia, which overexpress the inflammatory cytokine interleukin-1 (IL-1), and astrocytes, which overexpress the astrocyte-derived growth factor S100B are activated. It is thought that IL-1 and S100B cause the changes that ultimately define Alzheimer's disease.

Three genes on chromosome 21 have been implicated as contributing factors in Down syndrome as well as Alzheimer's disease. The gene for beta-amyloid precursor protein (ßAPP), which is the precursor protein for the amyloid-beta protein, is found on chromosome 21. Also found on

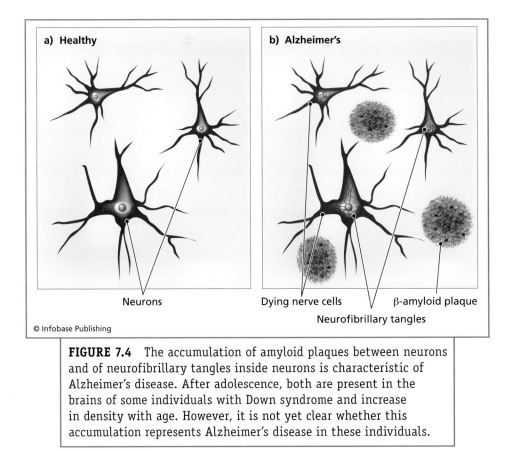

a) Healthy

b) Alzheimer's

Neurons

Dying nerve cells

β-amyloid plaque

Neurofibrillary tangles

© Infobase Publishing

FIGURE 7.4 The accumulation of amyloid plaques between neurons and of neurofibrillary tangles inside neurons is characteristic of Alzheimer's disease. After adolescence, both are present in the brains of some individuals with Down syndrome and increase in density with age. However, it is not yet clear whether this accumulation represents Alzheimer's disease in these individuals.

chromosome 21 is the gene for the enzyme superoxide dismutase, SOD1, and the gene for the astrocyte-derived neurotrophic factor S100B. Although deposition of Aß fibers in the brains of individuals with Down syndrome does not occur before adolescence, more subtle changes in Aß uptake and recycling occur as early as the 28th week of gestation. Overexpression of S100B occurs in the brain of fetuses with Down syndrome and progressively increases throughout the life of an individual with Down syndrome.

The gene for the cytokine interleukin-1 (IL-1) is not located on chromosome 21, but it is thought that IL-1 overexpression is induced by one or more genes on chromosome 21. Both ßAPP and S100B have been implicated in overexpression of IL-1 in both Alzheimer's disease and in Down syndrome. Overexpression of IL-1 is present in the brain of fetuses with Down syndrome and throughout adult life. In turn, IL-1 induces additional expression of ßAPP and S100B, so that their levels exceed the 150% level that would be expected to result from trisomy. Since IL-1 is a key player in the progression of changes that culminate in Alzheimer's disease, it is thought that it may also contribute to the development of Alzheimer disease in individuals with Down syndrome.

A key player in the inflammatory response, IL-1 is thought to be involved in a number of other diseases besides Alzheimer's disease. Certain nutrients can directly or indirectly activate transcription factors that regulate specific genes. Polyunsaturated fatty acids and antioxidants have been shown to regulate genes involved in the inflammatory response. Supplementing with the proper nutrients may therefore have the potential for reducing some of the negative effects caused by IL-1 overexpression.

Caution must be exercised in assigning a diagnosis of Alzheimer's disease to a person with Down syndrome. Thyroid problems, depression, or vitamin deficiencies can cause symptoms that can be mistaken for Alzheimer's disease. In addition, it is not yet certain whether the brain pathology found in Down syndrome is identical to that found in Alzheimer's patients. It also cannot be assumed that Alzheimer's disease is an inevitable outcome with Down syndrome. Many individuals with Down syndrome who are now past age 50 do not have dementia.

8

INTERVENTIONS AND TREATMENTS

Early intervention is the key to maximizing the potential of a child with Down syndrome. A number of interventions have been developed that are lessening the effects of the extra genetic material of trisomy 21. Most of these therapies produce the most benefit when begun during infancy and continued as long as needed, sometimes into adulthood. Each new generation of individuals with Down syndrome is experiencing better health, longer lives, and heightened accomplishments as a result of these interventions. Their success stories are teaching us that we can modify the effects of genes on health and development.

NUTRITIONAL THERAPIES

A number of vitamins, minerals, and amino acids have been found in various studies to be deficient in individuals with Down syndrome. This is most likely caused directly or indirectly by the overexpression of genes on chromosome 21. Nutritional therapy was an important component of the whole-body approach used by pediatrician Jack Warner in his work with children with Down syndrome until his death in 2004. Warner was inspired by the work of Henry Turkel, who developed a "U series" formula, which was a combination of nutrients and medications to counteract the effects of metabolic errors, including the overexpression of superoxide dismutase, in Down syndrome. Warner developed a supplement he called High Achievement Potential capsules, better known as HAP Caps, that was approved in 1986 by the U.S. Food and Drug Administration (FDA). HAP Caps contain the amino acids L-glutamine, tyrosine, and taurine; the vitamins A, C, E and B complex; the bioflavanoids rutin and quercetin; and the minerals selenium, zinc, manganese, copper, iron, cobalt, molybdenum, and iodine. Digestive enzymes, which are reduced in Down syndrome, are also a part of the HAP Caps formula. Coenzyme Q-10, an additional antioxidant, was added to the formula in 1996. Also recommended were flaxseed oil and dimethylglycine (DMG), a nutrient found in rice hulls. Thyroid function was monitored every 6 months up to 4 years and then yearly thereafter, with thyroxine given as indicated. Warner's clinic also used physical therapy and vision therapy to help prevent some of the motor and visual problems often seen with Down syndrome.

John Unruh gave a firsthand account of the children he saw at Warner's clinic, which was called the Warner House. He observed that as a group they had less of the typical appearance of Down syndrome and did not have the usual health problems. Their physical stature, academic success, and behavior were greater than he had observed in other groups of children with Down syndrome.

Robert Thiel analyzed changes in height, weight, nose bridge development, epicanthal fold, and facial swelling in a randomly drawn sample of patient files from the Warner House. He found that height was increased above the usual average for children with Down syndrome by 10.5% in a group of 36 females and 14.2% in a group of 48 males. Weight was slightly less (1.6%) than the usual average for a group of 40 females, and 8.5% greater than the usual average for a group of 50 males. Improvement in nose bridge development was increased by 34.6% in a group of 37 females and 30.7% in a group of 45 males. Extent of epicanthal fold improved an average of 29.6% in a group of 38 females and 34.4% in a group of 43 males. Facial swelling improved an average of 28.8% in a group of 39 females and 57.6% in a group of 46 males.

Dixie Lawrence Tafoya, an adoption agency director who adopted a child with Down syndrome, became interested in nutritional therapy for Down syndrome when the name of a child with Down syndrome that she was familiar with kept

INFANT STIMULATION

Infant stimulation, in addition to other early interventions, is strongly recommended for infants with Down syndrome. Not only is infant stimulation beneficial to all babies, but it may help prevent the slowing in brain development that is sometimes seen in young children with Down syndrome. Sensory stimulation was first observed in the 1960s by Mark Rosenzweig and colleagues at the University of California at Berkeley to increase the weight and number of connections in the brains of rats that were reared in an enriched environment with objects of various shapes, sizes, and colors that were changed frequently.

At birth, a baby has most of the neurons he or she will ever have. During the first 3 years of life, the weight of the brain triples, primarily from the formation of connections between neurons. It is the stimuli and the experiences the baby is exposed to during this time that determine where and how many of these connections, or synapses, between neurons will form. Although appearing on the honor roll. Tafoya found that he was one of his school's top students, could spell any word he knew as quickly backwards as forwards, and had few Down syndrome features. After finding out that these results had been achieved by his family's use of Turkel's formula, she contacted Turkel in Israel, and he referred her to Warner. After inviting Warner's team to Baton Rouge to meet with her and a group of families who also had children with Down syndrome, Tafoya developed her own modified protocol for her adopted daughter. Tafoya's protocol combined components of both Turkel's and Warner's protocols, with the addition of more vitamin C, extra zinc, extra vitamin B-6, extra amino

the brain reaches 95% of its adult size by age 4, brain development continues through the teen years, and synapse formation continues through adulthood. Stimulation of the brain by continuing to learn things has also been shown to slow the process of aging.

Infant stimulation involves engaging all of a baby's senses to optimize his or her ability to learn. Crib mobiles, large graphics, and brightly colored objects are often used. Sound stimulation can include things such as wind chimes, music, and talking, singing, or reading to the baby. Textures, massage, and safe temperature changes help develop the sense of touch. Taste and smell can be developed by exposure to novel or distinctive tastes and smells, while the parent describes them and gives them names. Outdoor excursions also expose the infant to sensory stimuli and learning experiences. Providing a baby with abundant early learning experiences that involve all the senses appears to confer an advantage in later learning.

acids, and the "smart drug" piracetam (in combination with vitamin B5 and phosphatidylcholine). She reported that children who were started on a metabolic formula in early infancy have few of the physical signs and developmental delays typically associated with Down syndrome. Treatment of babies in utero (during pregnancy) by supplements taken by the mother has also been reported. The physician who delivered one of them refused to believe that the baby had Down syndrome until he was shown the genetic analysis. MSB Plus and later NutriVene-D are two popular metabolic therapy formulas that were developed by Tafoya and are commercially available.

Geneticist and pediatrician Larry Leichtman uses the NutriVene-D formula in what he calls Targeted Nutritional Intervention (TNI) with the patients he sees at his clinic in Virginia Beach, Virginia. He conducted a seven-year study in which he compared the development of children with Down syndrome given the formula with those who took a multivitamin supplement only. Children who were given the formula were significantly higher in growth, IGA hormone levels, white blood cell counts, expressive and receptive language, and both fine and gross motor development compared to the children given the multivitamin supplement only. They also had significantly lower incidences of ear infections, upper respiratory infections, and gastroenteritis.

THYROID HORMONE MONITORING

Thyroid hormone supplementation individualized for the child with Down syndrome to bring thyroid hormone levels within the normal range is an important early intervention that should be continued through adulthood if indicated. Warner recommended that the T4 level be maintained at at least 8.5 µg/dl (micrograms per deciliter). Since T3 stimulates the synthesis of growth hormone, one of the ways hypothyroidism may slow growth is through reduction of growth hormone levels. Some children with Down syndrome have been given growth hormone injections to stimulate growth. Growth spurts have been reported, but it is not yet known what the long-term effects are.

PHYSICAL THERAPY

Physical therapy is important to prevent compensatory abnormal movements in response to the hypotonia, laxity of ligaments, and reduced muscular strength often found in children with Down syndrome. Appropriate exercises begun at an early age help prevent a waddling gait, stiffened knees, and difficulty in running as the children get older. Physical therapist Ardith Meyer recommends that babies with Down syndrome start physical therapy as early as 8 days of age.

Physical therapists use a variety of innovative techniques, many of which are modeled after play. These techniques help infants and toddlers as well as older children strengthen their muscles and improve their motor coordination. Dale Uhlrich and his research team at the University of Michigan found that infants with Down syndrome who practiced walking (with a parent's assistance) on a slow treadmill five days per week for eight minutes each day began to walk independently 3½ months earlier on average than those who did not. However, some therapists do not think the treadmill therapy is a good idea unless the baby has already mastered crawling. They believe that a child should master crawling and creeping before walking for proper neurological development.

SPEECH THERAPY

Hypotonia of the muscles involved in speech should be addressed at an early age by speech therapy. Speech development, language skills, and conversational skills are also addressed in speech therapy. Since speech production is difficult and progresses slowly for many children with Down syndrome, sessions with a speech therapist as well as related activities designed for home use are important in helping them develop their communication skills. Although there may be weekly sessions with a speech therapist as well as related activities designed for home use, the real work in speech therapy is done at home. Talking to the child, playing videos, audio recordings, and other media should be part of a normal routine.

FIGURE 8.1 A clinician works with a child in a speech therapy clinic.

Speech therapist Sarah Rosenfeld-Johnson believes that feeding intervention from birth onward is important in helping the mouth structures to develop properly. When the feeding position of an infant with Down syndrome allows the ears to be lower than the mouth, bottle milk can enter the middle ear because of the low muscle tone in the Eustachian tube. In addition, the baby's tongue protrudes to regulate the flow of milk through the bottle nipple, which usually has a larger than normal opening. This results in chronic otitis media, respiratory infections, and open-mouth breathing. Rosenfeld-Johnson has found that through the use of feeding intervention measures, including feeding the baby with Down syndrome in an upright position, this series of abnormal compensatory patterns can be avoided.

NEUROLOGICAL REHABILITATION THERAPY

Developmental psychologist John Unruh recommends enriching the environment of the child with Down syndrome with sensory stimulation and activities that encourage the normal development of the child's nervous system. It is important that these activities begin while the brain is still developing and can benefit the most from this type of therapy. In his book *Down Syndrome*, Unruh lists activities to be implemented in stages from birth onward. These activities address mobility development, speech and language development, vision, and tactile (touch) awareness.

For mobility development, Unruh recommends activities that ensure that the child moves through the normal crawling and creeping postures and movements so that the related pathways in the nervous system develop properly. For speech and language development, he recommends stimulating the child's mouth, lips, and tongue and enriching the child's environment with music, conversation, recorded voices and stories, and toys that make noise. Recommendations for vision development include enrichment of the child's environment with things such as mobiles, Christmas tree twinkle lights (with random twinkling patterns), a well-lit aquarium, large and colorful toys, a well-lit environment during waking hours, and exposure to large pictures with details that increase in complexity as the child ages. Suggestions for increasing tactile awareness include lots of touching, frequent baths, massage, tickling, towel rubs, light poking, and exposure of the skin to different textures of fabric. Naming body parts as they are touched is also recommended.

VISION THERAPY

Vision therapy focuses on improving the function of the visual system. There are a number of vision problems that can interfere with good vision and, subsequently, learning. Refractive errors, such as farsightedness and nearsightedness, are among them. Other problems involve eye movements, visual perception, and visual memory. Problems with eye movement include problems with how the eyes work together (teaming problems) and how well the eyes follow a moving object (tracking). Eye teaming problems, such as strabismus ("crossed" eye), produce double vision and make it difficult for a child to develop accurate stereoscopic, or three-dimensional, vision.

A vision therapist uses a variety of methods to correct refractive errors and to retrain the brain centers involved in controlling eye movement. Eyeglasses or contact lenses are used for refractive errors. An eye patch may be used for **diplopia** (double vision). Special prism lenses are

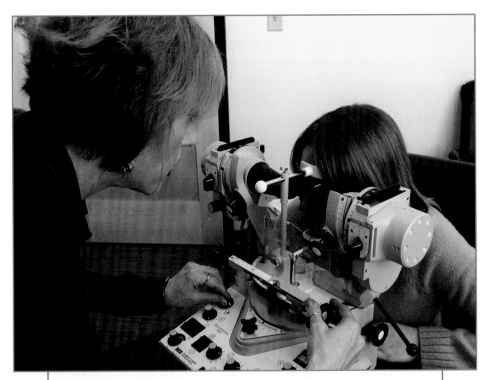

FIGURE 8.2 Orthoptics, or vision therapy, is used to correct visual impairments, uses a variety of eye exercises to improve vision. Problems such as strabismus (crossed eyes), convergence (tracking) problems, and accommodation (focusing) problems are addressed by both innovative manual and computerized techniques.

sometimes used to improve depth perception. Eye exercises are used to correct teaming and tracking errors as well as to improve depth perception. Specially designed computer programs are used to improve visual perception and visual memory.

Because it is the last sense to develop, vision may be more susceptible to metabolic imbalances, the effects of which are more noticeable after birth. Vision is also our most highly developed sense, with about 75% of the information we learn received through the eyes. Correction of visual problems is therefore vitally important in helping a child with Down syndrome reach his or her full potential.

RNA INTERFERENCE (RNAi)

RNA interference is a term used to describe the silencing of a specific gene by injecting double-stranded RNA with a nucleotide sequence that matches the target gene. It is being researched as a potential type of gene therapy. In 2001, it was shown in several studies that short synthetic double-stranded RNA molecules consisting of 21 to 22 nucleotides were able to silence a target mammalian gene. It is not yet completely understood how RNA interference works, but it is known that the short interfering RNAs (siRNAs) are incorporated into a complex of proteins known as the RNA-induced silencing complex (RISC). This complex is guided to the target mRNA by a complementary strand of siRNA. An endonuclease associated with the silencing complex then cuts the target mRNA, silencing the gene by preventing its translation into its protein product.

Several preclinical studies in animals have been done to investigate the therapeutic potential of RNA interference. A few clinical trials have begun, including one in which an siRNA is injected into the eye as treatment for macular degeneration. A lot of questions have been raised concerning the long-term safety of this therapy, which has sometimes proven toxic and even fatal in animal models after long-term administration. Moral and ethical questions have also been raised about the procedure. Some worry that average physical characteristics or intelligence could eventually be considered subnormal. At that point, gene therapy would have progressed into genetic engineering.

Other people have objections to gene therapy based on their religious beliefs.

A number of genes are overexpressed in Down syndrome, so questions remain about whether RNA interference would reduce the effect of some of these extra genes. However, the complex interplay of even one of these genes with genes on other chromosomes makes it difficult to predict the effects of gene silencing. There is always the risk of an immune response, and the immune system of a person with Down syndrome is already more vulnerable. Another worry that accompanies gene therapy is whether the viral vector that carries the siRNA could itself cause disease. RNA interference is still experimental, and the answers about its effects and its safety may be years down the road.

EXPECTATION AND OPPORTUNITY

A multidisciplinary approach that addresses all of the physical and developmental needs of a child with Down syndrome has been shown to be the most effective use of early interventions. The child's parents and the professionals they work with become a team to help the child with Down syndrome reach his or her maximum potential. However, the most important components of an early intervention program are the expectations the parents and professionals have for the child and the opportunities the child is given to learn and develop. A child with Down syndrome should be surrounded with all the stimulation, activities, and learning opportunities that one would provide any child.

GLOSSARY

Albinism   Condition in which the pigment melanin is missing.

Amblyopia   Partial blindness caused by preferential use of one eye, as in strabismus. "Lazy eye."

Amino Acid   The molecule specified by a codon. Amino acids are linked together to form peptides, polypeptides, and proteins. They also serve as components of coenzymes and precursors for other molecules.

Aneuploidy   A change in the number of chromosomes in one or more chromosome pairs.

Atrial septal defect   An opening in the septum between the atria of the heart.

Atrioventricular septal defect   A large opening in the septum of the heart that involves both the atria and the ventrcles.

Autoradiogram   Photograph prepared by exposing undeveloped film to radiolabeled probes bound to DNA or RNA fragments or polypeptides (protein fragments) separated by gel electrophoresis.

Brushfield spots   Small white spots on the iris of the eye. Often seen in individuals with Down syndrome.

Cell adhesion molecules   Transmembrane (membrane-spanning) proteins that connect cells to each other. Important in organ formation during embryonic development.

Chromatin   DNA and protein complex of which chromosomes are made.

Chromosome   A bundle of DNA and proteins that contain an organism's genetic information.

Codon   A triplet of nucleotides that specifies an amino acid or a start or stop sequence that precedes or follows the codon sequence for a protein.

Complementary   Having an opposite, pairing sequence of nucleotides.

Crossing over   Exchange of sequences between two nonsister chromatids of a chromosome tetrad during meiosis.

Cytoplasm   Thick, semiliquid substance that fills the interior of the cell outside the nucleus.

Deoxyribonucleic acid (DNA)   Molecule consisting of two nucleotide chains linked by hydrogen bonds and twisted in a spiral around each other. Contains the genetic, or hereditary, information.

Diplopia   Double vision.

DNA fingerprinting   Technique in which noncoding sequences in DNA samples are compared to identify a person or establish paternity.

DNA microarray   Technique used to study the expression of genes in cells and tissues.

DNA repair   Repair of damage to DNA by direct chemical reversal of damage or by excision and replacement of a base or nucleotide.

DNA replication   Duplication of DNA during mitosis or meiosis.

DNA sequences   A succession of letters representing the primary structure of a real or hypothetical DNA molecule or strand.

Double helix   Shape of DNA in which two helices, or coils, of DNA joined by hydrogen bases spiral around each other.

Endocardial cushion defect Atrioventricular septal defect.

Enzyme Protein that catalyzes a chemical reaction without itself being changed.

Epicanthal fold A fold of skin that covers the inner corner of the eye.

Euploidy Condition in which cells have a different number of complete copies of all the chromosomes.

Excision repair Type of DNA repair in which a base or nucleotide is removed and replaced.

Exon Region of a gene that codes for a portion of a particular protein and is transcribed into mRNA.

Gel electophoresis Separation of DNA, RNA, or protein fragments of different sizes by migration in response to an electric field across the length of a gel.

Gene A DNA segment containing the genetic code for one particular protein and the regulatory regions necessary for its transcription.

Gene expression Process by which a gene is transcribed into mRNA and then translated into a protein. Some genes are transcribed into transfer RNA or ribosomal RNA and are not translated into a protein product. This is also considered gene expression.

Hypothyroidism Condition caused by an underactive thyroid gland.

Hypotonia Low muscle tone.

Interphase Stage between cell divisions in which the chromatin is extended. Replication occurs during this stage.

Intron Segment of DNA between exons that is spliced out of the pre-mRNA transcript before mRNA is translated.

Karyotype A laboratory test to identify the number, size, and shape of an individual's chromosomes.

Meiosis   Type of cell division in which the nucleus divides twice to produce reproductive cells with one chromosome from each pair.

Metabolic error   Defect in an enzyme that disrupts a metabolic pathway or causes it to be abnormal.

Mitosis   Type of cell division that results in two identical daughter cells with a complete set of chromosome pairs.

Monosomy   Condition in which only one of a particular pair of chromosomes is present.

Mosaicism   Condition in which some cells have a different chromosome number than other cells.

Multiple marker tests   Prenatal screening tests in which the levels of certain proteins in the mother's blood are measured.

Mutagen   Chemical or other agent that causes a mutation.

Mutation   Change in a gene or a chromosome.

Myelin   Fatty layered covering that provides insulation that enhances the speed of electrical impulses traveling down an axon.

Myelination   Formation of a sheath, or covering, of myelin around a nerve fiber.

Nondisjunction   Failure of chromatids to separate in mitosis or of chromosomes to separate in meiosis.

Nucleotide   Basic unit of DNA and RNA; composed of a nitrogenous base, a sugar, and a phosphate group.

Organelle   Specialized intracellular structure found in the cytoplasm. Performs essential functions for the cell. Examples include the nucleus, mitochondria, endoplasmic reticulum, and ribosomes.

Otitis media   Inflammation or infection of the middle ear accompanied by fluid buildup.

Palmar crease   Single, deep crease across the palm of the hand. Also called a simian crease.

Palpebral fissues   Openings of the eyes.

Peptide   A chain of two or more amino acids.

Phenylketonuria   Metabolic disorder in which the amino acid phenylalanine is not metabolized correctly.

Plantar crease   Deep, vertical crease in the sole of the foot.

Polymerase chain reaction   Laboratory technique used to replicate a small sample of DNA millions of times.

Probe   Fragment of DNA or RNA or an antibody that is radiolabeled or tagged with a fluorescent or other marker and that can bind with complementary DNA or RNA fragments or a protein to identify them.

Purine   Nitrogenous base with two rings of carbon and nitrogen atoms; adenine and guanine are purines.

Regulatory protein   Protein that regulates a body function.

Ribonucleic acid (RNA)   Nucleic acid that is usually single-stranded, has ribose instead of deoxyribose as the sugar component, and exists in several forms that function to copy (transcribe) DNA and translate it into protein products.

Ribosome   Complex of proteins and RNA where mRNA is translated into protein.

Southern blot   Transfer of DNA or RNA fragments or polypeptides from a gel after electrophoresis to a nylon membrane, where a probe is applied in preparation for an autoradiogram.

Strabismus   Condition in which one or both eyes turns in or out; caused by problems with the brain centers that control eye movements.

Structural protein   Protein of which a body structure is composed.

Subluxation   Partial disclocation of the joints.

Superoxide dismutase   Enzyme that catalyzes the breakdown of the superoxide free radical into hydrogen peroxide and oxygen.

Thyroid-stimulating hormone   Hormone released into the bloodstream by the pituitary gland that stimulates the thyroid gland to produce thyroid hormones.

Transcript   Messenger RNA copy of a DNA sequence.

Transcription   Process by which an mRNA copy of the nucleotide sequence of a gene is made for the purpose of translation into the protein product of the gene.

Transcription factors   Proteins that influence the expression of a gene by binding to a regulatory sequence on the DNA molecule.

Translation   The process by which the messenger RNA transcript is "read"and a protein molecule is produced.

Translocation   Process in which a chromosomal segment transfers to a member of a different chromosome pair.

Transport protein   Protein that assists in the transport of molecules in the body.

Trisomy   Condition in which three copies of chromosome 21 are present. Occurs in 95% of individuals with Down syndrome.

Trisomy 21   Down syndrome; condition in which three copies of chromosome 21 are present.

Vector   A self-replicating chromosome of a bacteria or virus into which a DNA fragment is inserted for purposes of replication.

Ventricular defect   Opening in the septum of the heart between the ventricles.

BIBLIOGRAPHY

All About Vision. "Eye Problems and Diseases," Available online. URL: http://www.allaboutvision.com/conditions/.

Armstrong, W. P. "Polymerase Chain Reaction (PCR)," Palomar College, Life Sciences. Available online. URL: http://waynesword.palomar.edu/lmexer3b.htm.

Arnaud, Celia Henry. "Delivering RNA Interference: Developing siRNA therapeutics depends on synthetic delivery systems," *Chemical and Engineering News* (November 13, 2006). Available online. URL: http://pubs.acs.org/cen/coverstory/84/8446cover.html.

ASSID 2007 Conference. "Keynote Speakers: Ruth Cromer," Australian Society for the Study of Intellectual Disability. Available online. URL: http://www.strongercommunities.curtin.edu.au/assid2007/keynotes.htm.

Augustine, E.C. and R.M. Macleod. "Prolactin and growth hormone synthesis: effects of perphenazine, alpha-methyltyrosine and estrogen in different thyroid states." *Proceedings of the Society for Experimental Biology and Medicine* 150 (1975): 551–556.

Baciewicz, F.A. Jr., W.S. Melvin, D. Basilius, and J.T. Davis. "Congenital heart disease in Down's syndrome patients: a decade of surgical experience." Thoracic and Cardiovascular Surgery 37 (1989): 369–371.

Barlow, G.M., X.N. Chen, Z.Y. Shi, G.E. Lyons, D.M. Kurnit, L. Celle, N.B. Spinner, et al. "Down syndrome congenital heart disease: a narrowed region and a candidate gene." *Genetics Medicine* 3 (2001): 91–101.

BBC News. "Down's Life Expectancy Doubles." Available online. URL: http://news.bbc.co.uk/1/hi/health/1884178.stm.

Bernal, J.E., and I. Briceno. "Genetic and other diseases in the pottery of Tumaco-La Tolita culture in Colombia-Ecuador." Clinical Genetics 70 (2006): 188–191.

The Biology Web. "Meiosis." Clinton Community College. Available online. URL: http://faculty.clintoncc.suny.edu/faculty/ Michael.Gregory/files/Bio%20101/Bio%20101%20Lectures/ Meiosis/meiosis.htm.

Bray, I., D.E. Wright, C. Davies, and E.B.Hook. "Joint estimation of down syndrome risk and ascertainment rates: A meta-analysis of nine published data sets." *Prenatal Diagnosis* (1998) 18: 9–20.

Bucci I., G. Napolitano, C. Giuliani, S. Lio, A. Minnucci, F. Di Giacomo, G. Calabrese, G. Sabatino, G. Palka, and F. Monaco. "Zinc sulfate supplementation improves thyroid function in hypozincemic Down children." *Biology of Trace Elements Research* 67 (1999): 257–68.

Carpi, Anthony. "DNA and Protein Synthesis," Science Classes. Available online. URL: http://web.jjay.cuny.edu/~acarpi/ NSC/12-dna.htm.

Chen, Harold, and Jessica B. Johnson. "Down Syndrome," eMedicineHealth. Available online. URL: http://www. emedicinehealth.com/down_syndrome/article_em.htm.

Chrisburke.org. "Chris Burke with Joe and John DeMasi Official Site," Available online. URL: http://www.chrisburke. org/index.php.

Colorado State University. "Cell Adhesion Molecules," Available online. URL: http://www.vivo.colostate.edu/hbooks/ cmb/cells/pmemb/adhesion.html.

"Current Perspectives on Down Syndrome: Selected Medical and Social Issues." *American Journal of Medical Genetics*

Part C (Seminars in Medical Genetics) 142C (2006): 127–130.

Dale, Jeremy W., and Malcolm von Schantz. *Genes to Genomes: Concepts and Applications of DNA Technology.* Chichester, England: John Wiley & Sons, 2002.

De la Luna, S., and X. Estivill. "Cooperation to amplify gene-dosage-imbalance effects." *Trends in Molecular Medicine* 12 (2006): 451–454.

Dierssen, Mara, Jon Ortiz-Abalia, Glòria Arqué, Maria Martinez de Lagrán, and Cristina Fillat. "Pitfalls and Hopes in Down Syndrome Therapeutic Approaches: In the Search for Evidence-Based Treatments." *Behavior Genetics* 36 (2006): 454–468.

Dixon, Natalia, Priya S. Kishnani, and Sherri Zimmerman. "Clinical Manifestations of Hematologic and Oncologic Disorders in Patients with Down Syndrome." *American Journal of Medical Genetics Part C (Seminars in Medical Genetics)* 142C (2006): 149–157.

Dutta, Samikshan, Krishnadas Nandagopal, Prasanta Kumar Gangopadhyay, and Kanchan Mukhopadhyay. "Molecular Aspects of Down Syndrome," *Indian Pediatrics* 42 (2005): 339–344. Available online. URL: http://www.indianpediatrics. net/apr2005/339.pdf

Early Parent Intervention Project (ARC Texas). "General Sensory Stimulation for Infants," The Colorado Springs Down Syndrome Association. Available online. URL: http://www. csdsa.org/artthera.asp.

Eisenhaber, Frank, and Alexander Schleiffer. "Gregor Mendel: The Beginning of Biomathematics," Research Institute of Molecular Pathology (IMP) Bioinformatics Group. Available online. URL: http://mendel.imp.ac.at/mendeljsp/biography/ biography.jsp.

Felton, James S. "Food Mutagens." Lawrence Livermore National Laboratory, Molecular Toxicology Group. Available online. URL: http://www.llnl.gov/str/Food_Mutagens.intro. html.

Felton, James S. "The Cooking Makes a Difference." Lawrence Livermore National Laboratory, Molecular Toxicology Group. Available online. URL: http://www.llnl.gov/str/ FoodSection3.html.

Ferrando-Miguel, R., M.S. Cheon, J.W. Yang, and G. Lubec. "Overexpression of transcription factor BACH1 in fetal Down syndrome brain." *Journal of Neural Transmission Supplement* 67 (2003): 193–205.

Findlay, Vanessa. "Treadmill Helps Down Syndrome Kids to Walk," ABC Science Online (November 9, 2001). Available online. URL: http://www.abc.net.au/science/news/stories/ s412504.htm.

Fouad, Tamer. "Glutathione peroxidase enzyme," DoctorsLounge.com. Available online. URL: http://www. doctorslounge.com/primary/articles/antioxidants/ antioxidants9.htm.

Fowkes, Steven W. "An Interview with Dixie Lawrence," Cognitive Enhancement Research Institute. *Smart Drug News* (July 18, 1994). Available online. URL: http://www.ceri.com/ dixie.htm.

Fowkes, Steven W., and Ward Dean. "Smart Drugs and Down's Syndrome," Cognitive Enhancement Research Institute. *Smart Drug News* (February 14, 1994). Available online. URL: http://www.ceri.com/downs1.htm.

Frank, L. "People With Down Syndrome Appear to Have Genes That Protect Against Cancer," Genome News Network. Available online. URL: http://www.genomenewsnetwork. org/articles/04_00/downs_cancer.shtml.

Freeman, S.B., L.F. Taft, K.J. Dooley, K. Allran, S.L. Sherman, T.J. Hassold, M.J. Khoury, and D.M. Saker. "Population-based study of congenital heart defects in Down syndrome." *American Journal of Medical Genetics* 80 (1998): 213–217.

Gardiner, Kathleen, and Alberto C.S. Costa. "The Proteins of Human Chromosome 21." *American Journal of Medical Genetics Part C (Seminars in Medical Genetics)* 142C: 196–205 (2006).

Genomics.energy.gov. "Gene therapy." Human Genome Project Information. Available online. URL: http://www.ornl.gov/sci/techresources/Human_Genome/medicine/genetherapy.shtml#3.

Golder N., and W.C. Cooley. Preventive Management of Children with Congenital Anomalies and Syndromes. Cambridge: Cambridge University Press, 2000.

Goldstein, Jill M., David N. Kennedy, and Verne S. Caviness Jr. "Images in Neuroscience: Brain Development, XI, Sexual Dimorphism." *American Journal of Psychiatry* 156 (1999): 352. Available online. URL: http://ajp.psychiatryonline.org/cgi/reprint/156/3/352.

Graham, Judith. "What We Know About How Children Learn." University of Maine Cooperative Extension. Available online. URL: http://www.umext.maine.edu/onlinepubs/htmpubs/4356.htm.

Griffin, W. Sue T. "Inflammation and neurodegenerative diseases." American Journal of Clinical Nutrition 83 (suppl) (2006): 470S–474S.

Griffiths, Anthony, J.F., William M. Gelbart, Jeffrey H. Miller, and Richard C. Lewontin. *Modern Genetic Analysis.* New York: W.H. Freeman, 1999.

Groleau, Rick. "How Cells Divide: Mitosis vs. Meiosis." NOVA Online. Public Broadcasting System. Available online. URL: http://www.pbs.org/wgbh/nova/miracle/divide.html.

Haiken, Melanie. "A New Day for Kids With Down's," alternativemedicine.com.Availableonline.URL:http://www. alternativemedicine.com/common/news/store_news. asp?task=store_news&SID_store_news=230&storeID= 02AD61F001A74B5887D3BD11F6C28169.

Hammerle B., A. Carnicero, C. Elizalde, J. Ceron, S. Martinez, and F.J. Tejedor. "Expression Patterns and Subcellular Localization of the Down Syndrome Candidate Protein MNB/DYRK1A Suggest a Role in Late Neuronal Differentiation," Eur J Neurosci 17 (2003): 2277-2286. Available online. URL: http://www.ds-health.com/abst/a0311.htm.

Hattori, M., A. Fujiyama, T.D. Taylor, H. Watanabe, T. Yada, H.S. Park, A. Toyoda et al. "The DNA sequence of human chromosome 21." *Nature* 407 (2000): 110.

Hunter, Alasdair G.W. "Down Syndrome," in *Management of Genetic Syndromes,* 2nd ed. Suzanne B. Cassidy and Judith E. Allanson, eds. Hoboken, New Jersey: Wiley-Liss, Inc. 2005, 191–210.

Jorde, L.B., J.C. Carey, M.J. Bamshad, and R.L. White. Medical Genetics, 3rd ed., St. Louis, MO: Mosby, 2006.

Kantor, M.D. "Eye Movements—Uncontrollable," MedlinePlus Encyclopedia. National Institutes of Health. Available online. URL: http://www.nlm.nih.gov/medlineplus/ency/ article/003037.htm.

Kimball, John W. "DNA Repair." Kimball's Biology Pages, Harvard College. Available online. URL: http://users.rcn.com/ jkimball.ma.ultranet/BiologyPages/D/DNArepair.html.

———. "DNA Sequencing." Kimball's Biology Pages, Harvard College. Available online. URLhttp://users.rcn.com/ jkimball.ma.ultranet/BiologyPages/D/DNAsequencing.html.

———. "Endoreplication." Kimball's Biology Pages, Harvard College. Available online. URL: http://users.rcn.com/jkimball.ma.ultranet/BiologyPages/E/Endoreplication.html.

————. "The Extracellular Matrix (ECM)." Kimball's Biology Pages, Harvard College. Available online. URL: http://users.rcn.com/jkimball.ma.ultranet/BiologyPages/E/ECM.html.

Kimball, John W. "Gene Expression: Transcription." Kimball's Biology Pages, Harvard College. Available online. URL: http://users.rcn.com/jkimball.ma.ultranet/BiologyPages/T/Transcription.html

Klitsch, Michael. "Mercy or Murder? Ethical Dilemmas in Newborn Care." *Family Planning Perspectives* 15 (1983): 143–146.

Korenberg, J.R., C. Bradley, and C.M. Distechet. "Down Syndrome: Molecular Mapping of the Congenital Heart Disease and Duodenal Stenosis." *American Journal of Human Genetics* 50 (1992): 294–302.

Kornman, Kenneth S. "Interleukin 1 genetics, inflammatory mechanisms, and nutrigenetic opportunities to modulate diseases of aging." *American Journal of Clinical Nutrition* 83 (suppl) (2006): 475S–483S.

Kozma, Chaira. "What Are the Medical Problems Associated With Down Syndrome?" downsyn.com. Available online. URL: http://www.downsyn.com/whatmed.php.

Kumin, Libby. "Comprehensive Speech and Language Treatment for Infants, Toddlers, and Children with Down Syndrome." Down Syndrome: Health Issues. Available online. URL: http://www.ds-health.com/speech.htm.

Lane, Kerry S. Tobacco Commission. "Monitoring and Remediation of Aflatoxin and Mycotoxin Levels on Tobacco as a Harm Reduction Strategy." University of North Texas Libraries, Government Documents. Available online. URL: http://govinfo.library.unt.edu/tobacco/disc/disc18.htm.

Leichtman, Lawrence G. "Targeted Nutritional Intervention (TNI) in the Treatment of Children and Adults with Down Syndrome Principles Behind Its Use, Treatment Protocols, and an Expanded Bibliography," Genetics and Disabilities Diagnostic Care Center. Available online. URL: http://www.lleichtman.org/tni.shtml.

Lenhart, Harry. "First Specific Link To Congenital Heart Defect Identified." Oregon Health & Science University. Available online. URL: http://www.ohsu.edu/ohsuedu/newspub/releases/101706heart.cfm.

Leshin, Len. "Down Syndrome: Health Issues," Available online. URL: http://www.ds-health.com.

———. "Mosaic Down Syndrome." Down Syndrome: Health Issues. Available online. URL: http://www.ds-health.com/mosaic.htm.

Lessmann, Hans F. "Visual Enhancement for People with Down Syndrome." Vision Development Institute, 2003 Trisomy 21 Research Conference. Available online. URL: http://www.altonweb.com/cs/downsyndrome/lessmann.html.

Levitas, A.S., and C.S. Reid, "An Angel with Down Syndrome in a Sixteenth Century Flemish Nativity Painting." *American Journal of Medical Genetics* 116A (2003): 399–405.

Lewis, Edward B. "Thomas Hunt Morgan and His Legacy." NobelPrize.org. Available online. URL: http://nobelprize.org/nobel_prizes/medicine/articles/lewis/index.html.

Lewis, Rachel A. "Umbilical Hernia." University of Maryland Medical Center. Available online. URL: http://www.umm.edu/ency/article/000987.htm.

Lloyd, Robin. "Flies With the Right Stuff: Shuttle Experiment to Explore Astronaut Immunity." Space.com. Available online. URL: http://www.space.com/scienceastronomy/060627_science_tuesday.html.

Loe, Julie. "What Is Down Syndrome?" Pediatric Services. Available online. URL: http://www.pediatricservices.com/answers/006-down.htm.

Lombardi, Kate Stone. "Walking the Road of Life in the Face of a Disability." *The New York Times* (January 23, 1994). Available online. URL: http://query.nytimes.com/gst/fullpage.html?sec=health&res=9D06E2DD1530F930A15752C0A962958260.

Maas, Werner. *Gene Action: A Historical Account.* New York: Oxford University Press, 2001.

Marder, Liz. "Gastrointestinal Problems in Children with Down's Syndrome." The Down's Syndrome Medical Interest Group. Available online. URL: http://www.dsmig.org.uk/library/articles/gastro-article-marder.pdf.

Maroni, Gustavo. *Molecular and Genetic Analysis of Human Traits.* Malden, MA: Blackwell Science, Inc., 2001.

Martinez-Frias, M.L. "The Real Earliest Historical Evidence of Down Syndrome." *American Journal of Medical Genetics* 132A (2005): 231.

Maslen, Cheryl L. "Molecular genetics of atrioventricular septal defects." *Current Opinion in Cardiology* 19 (2006): 205–210.

Maslen, Cheryl L., Darcie Babcock, Susan W. Robinson, Lora J. H. Bean, Kenneth J. Dooley, Virgina L. Willour, and Stephanie L. Sherman. "CRELD1 Mutations Contribute to the Occurrence of Cardiac Atrioventricular Septal Defects in Down Syndrome," *American Journal of Medical Genetics* Part A 140A (2006): 2501–2505. Available online. URL: http://www.ohsu.edu/ohsuedu/newspub/releases/upload/MaslenDS.pdf.

May, Philip B. Jr. "Thyroid Dysfunction in Down Syndrome: Interpretation and Management of Different Patterns of Laboratory Abnormalities." Riverbend Down Syndrome

Parent Support Group. Available online. URL: http://www. altonweb.com/cs/downsyndromeindexhtm?page=thyroid may.html.

MedicineNet.com. "Leukemia." Available online. URL: http:// www.medicinenet.com/leukemia/article.htm.

Mediderm Laboratories, LLC. "More on Skin Pigmentation." Available online. URL: http://www.medidermlab.com/ pigmentation.htm.

Meiogen Biotechnology Corporation. "Interferon." Riverbend Down Syndrome Parent Support Group. Available online. URL: http://www.he.net/~altonweb/cs/downsyndrome/ interferon.html.

"Memory & Down Syndrome Abstracts." The Riverbend Down Syndrome Parent Support Group. Available online. URL: http:// www.altonweb.com/cs/downsyndrome/memoryab.html.

Mirkinson, A.E. "Is Down's Syndrome A Modern Disease?" *Lancet* 2 (1968): 103.

Montelone, Beth A. "Mutation, Mutagens, and DNA Repair." Kansas State University, Biology. Available online. URL: http://www-personal.k-state.edu/~bethmont/mutdes. html#mutagens.

Mrak, Robert E., and W. Sue T. Griffin. "Glia and their cytokines in progression of neurodegeneration." *Neurobiology of Aging* 26 (2005): 349–354.

———. "Trisomy 21 and the Brain." *Journal of Neuropathology and Experimental Neurology* 63 (2004): 679–685.

Nadel, Lynn, and Donna Rosenthal,.ed. *Down Syndrome: Living and Learning in the Community.* New York: Wiley-Liss, 1995.

Napolitano G, G. Palka, S. Grimaldi, C. Giuliani, G. Laglia, G. Calabrese, M.A. Satta, G. Neri, and F. Monaco. "Growth delay in Down syndrome and zinc sulphate supplementation." *American Journal of Medical Genetics Suppl.* (1990) 7:63–65.

National Center for Biotechnology Information. "Microarrays: Chipping Away at the Mysteries of Science and Medicine." Available online. URL: http://www.ncbi.nlm.nih.gov/About/primer/microarrays.html.

National Center for Human Genome Research, National Institutes of Health. "Polymerase Chain Reaction—Xeroxing DNA." AccessExcellence, National Health Museum. Available online. URL: http://www.accessexcellence.org/RC/AB/IE/PCR_Xeroxing_DNA.html.

New Mexico Institute of Mining and Technology. "How the DNA Sequencer Works." Available online. URL: http://infohost.nmt.edu/~biology/sequencer.htm.

Nobel.org. "Thomas H. Morgan: The Nobel Prize in Physiology or Medicine 1933." Available online. URL: http://nobelprize.org/nobel_prizes/medicine/laureates/1933/morgan-bio.html.

O'Neil, Dennis. "Mendel's Genetics." Behavioral Sciences Department, Palomar College. Available online. URL: http://anthro.palomar.edu/mendel/mendel_1.htm.

O'Shea, Karen. "A Push to Preserve Willowbrook's Legacy." *Staten Island Advance* (March 19, 2006). Available online. URL: http://www.csinews.net/IntheNews/March_06/19_Willowbrook.htm.

Pear, Robert. "Judge Strikes Rule Requiring Care for Infants With Defects." *The New York Times* (April 15, 1983). Available online. URL: http://query.nytimes.com/gst/fullpage.html?res=9C03E4DE1638F936A25757C0A965948260&sec=health&spon=&pagewanted=1.

Pinter, Joseph D., Stephan Eliez, J. Eric Schmitt, George T. Capone, and Allan L. Reiss. "Neuroanatomy of Down's Syndrome: A High-Resolution MRI Study," *American Journal of Psychiatry* 158 (2001):1659-1665. Available online. URL: http://ajp.psychiatryonline.org/cgi/reprint/158/10/1659.

Rachidi, Mohammed, Carmela Lopes, Giselle Charron, Anne-Lise Delezoide, Evelyne Paly, Bernard Bloch, and Jean-Maurice Delabar. "C21orf5, a human candidate gene for brain abnormalities and mental retardation in Down syndrome." *Cytogenetics and Genome Research* 112 (2006): 16–22.

———. "Spatial and temporal localization during embryonic and fetal human development of the transcription factor SIM2 in brain regions altered in Down syndrome." *International Journal of Developmental Neuroscience* 23 (2005): 475–484.

Rajantie, J. "Review: Leukemia in Down's Syndrome," *The Cancer Journal* 9 (1996): 121–123. Available online. URL: http://www.he.net/~altonweb/cs/downsyndrome/index. htm?page=rajantie.html.

Richards, B.W. "Is Down's Syndrome A Modern Disease?" *The Lancet* 2 (1968): 353–354.

Riverbend Down Syndrome Parent Support Group. "Down Syndrome Timeline." Available online. URL: http://www. altonweb.com/cs/downsyndrome/index.htm?page= timeline.html.

Rodriguez, M. "Ask a Geneticist: Why Is It That Older Women Are More Likely To Have Babies With Complications Like Down Syndrome Than Younger Women?" Understanding Genetics, TheTech.org. Available online. URL: http://www. thetech.org/genetics/ask.php?id=234.

Rosenfeld-Johnson, Sara. "The Oral-Motor Myths of Down Syndrome." Children's Academy for Neurodevelopment and Learning. Available online. URL: http://www.kidscanlearn. net/down.htm.

Roubertoux, P. I., and B. Kerdelhué. "Trisomy 21: From Chromosomes to Mental Retardation." *Behavior Genetics* 36 (2006): 346–354.

Rutgers University. "Chromosome numbers of different species." Available online. URL: http://morgan.rutgers.edu/morganwebframes/level1/page2/ChromNum.html.

Salleh, Anna. "Down Syndrome Life Expectancy Doubles." ABC Science Online (March 22, 2002). Available online. URL: http://www.abc.net.au/science/news/stories/s510389.htm.

Sanger, Frederick. "Autobiography." NobelPrize.org. Available online. URL: http://nobelprize.org/nobel_prizes/chemistry/laureates/1980/sanger-autobio.html.

Sedat Lab at UCSF. "Polytene Chromosomes." University of California at San Francisco. Available online. URL: http://www.ucsf.edu/sedat/polytene_chrom.html.

Seidman, J.G., and Christine Seidman. "Transcription Factor Haploinsufficiency: When Half a Loaf Is Not Enough." *Journal of Clinical Investigation* 109 (2002): 451–455. Available online. URL: http://www.pubmedcentral.nih.gov/picrender.fcgi?artid=150881&blobtype=pdf.

Shapiro, E., Herbert H. Samuels, and Barry M. Yaffe. "Thyroid and Glucocorticoid Hormones Synergistically Control Growth Hormone mRNA in Cultured GH1 Cells." *Proceedings of the National Academy of Sciences* 75 (1978): 45–49. Available online. URL: http://www.pubmedcentral.nih.gov/articlerender.fcgi?artid=411180.

Shaw, Christine. "One Mother's Hope, Another's Horror." Euthanasia.com. Available online. URL: http://www.euthanasia.com/downs.html.

Shott, Sally R. "Down Syndrome: Common Otolaryngologic Manifestations." *American Journal of Medical Genetics* Part C (Seminars in Medical Genetics) 142C (2006): 131–140.

Smith, Jeremy W., A. Tudor Evans, B. Costall, and James W. Smythe. "Thyroid hormones, brain function and cognition: a brief review." *Neuroscience and Biobehavioral Reviews* 26 (2002): 45–60.

Snustad, D.P., and M.J. Simmons. *Principles of Genetics,* 3rd ed., New York: John Wiley & Sons, 2003.

Stedman, D.J., and D.H. Eichorn. "A comparison of the growth and development of institutionalized and home-reared mongoloids during infancy and early childhood." *American Journal of Mental Deficiencies* 69 (1964): 391–401.

Steinberg, Jacques. "Opening a Window Despite a Disability," *The New York Times* (March 20, 1994). Available online. URL: http://query.nytimes.com/gst/fullpage.html?sec=health& res=9D07EED7173CF933A15750C0A962958260.

Stray-Gunderson, Karen, ed. *Babies with Down Syndrome: A New Parents Guide.* Bethesda, MD: Woodbine House, 1986.

Sturtevant, A.H. *A History of Genetics.* New York: Harper & Row, 1965

Strydom, Jan, and Susan du Plessis. "IQ Test: Where Does It Come From and What Does It Measure." Audioblox. Available online. URL: http://www.audiblox2000.com/dyslexia_ dyslexic/dyslexia014.htm.

Suurkula, Jaan. "Junk DNA." Physicians and Scientists for Responsible Application of Science and Technology. Available online. URL: http://www.psrast.org/junkdna.htm.

The Linus Pauling Institute. "Linus Pauling—Scientist for the Ages." Available online. URL:http://dwb.unl.edu/Teacher/

NSF/C04/C04Links/osu.orst.edu/dept/lpi/lpbio/lpbio2. html.

Thiel, R.J., and S.W. Fowkes. "Down syndrome and epilepsy: a nutritional connection?" *Medical Hypotheses* 62 (2004): 35–44.

Thiel, Robert J. "Facial Effects of the Warner Protocol for Children with Down Syndrome." *Journal of Orthomolecular Medicine* 17 (2002): 111–116. Available online. URL: http://www. warnerhouse.com/facial.htm.

———. "Growth Effects of the Warner Protocol for Children with Down Syndrome," Center for Natural Health Research. Available online. URL: http://www.healthresearch.com/ height.htm.

———. "Orthomolecular Therapy and Down Syndrome: Rationale and Clinical Results." Presentation at the 8th Annual Scientific (March 1, 2002) Program of the Orthomolecular Health-Medicine Society. Available online. URL: www. warnerhouse.com/orthods.htm

University at Buffalo School of Public Health and Health Professions. "Special Education Laws." Available online. URL: http://atto.buffalo.edu/registered/ATBasics/Foundation/ Laws/specialed.php.

University of Wisconsin-Madison. "Kids With Down Syndrome Learn Language Beyond Adolescence," *ScienceDaily*. Available online. URL: http://www.sciencedaily.com/releases/ 2002/10/021017065355.htm

Unruh, J.F. *Down Syndrome: Successful Parenting of Children with Down Syndrome,* Eugene, OR: Fern Ridge Press, 1994.

Unruh, John F. "What Is the Centre for Neurological Rehabilitation." The Centre for Neurological Rehabilitation. Available online. URL: http://www.thecnr.com/wcnr.htm.

Vicari, Stefano. "Motor Development and Neuropsychological Patterns in Persons with Down Syndrome." *Behavior Genetics* 36 (2006): 355–364.

Victorian Department of Human Services (Australia). "Gene therapy." Better Health Channel. Available online. URL: http://www.betterhealthchannel.com.au/bhcv2/bhcarticles.nsf/pages/Gene_therapy?open.

Volpe, E.P. "Is Down Syndrome a Modern Disease?" *Perspectives in Biology and Medicine* 29 (Part I, 1986): 423–436.

Ward, O.C. "Further Early Historical Evidence of Down Syndrome." *American Journal of Medical Genetics* 126A (2004): 220.

Warner House. Available online. URL: http://www.warnerhouse.com.

Washington, Reginald L. "Endocardial Cushion Defect (Atrioventricular Septal Defect)." Fairview Health Services. Available online. URL: http://www.fairview.org/healthlibrary/content/ca_ecushion_car.htm.

Wetzler, Cynthia Magriel. "Meeting the Challenge of Down Syndrome." *The New York Times,* (August 24, 1997). Available online. URL: http://query.nytimes.com/gst/fullpage.html?sec=health&res=9E06E7DC153EF937A1575BC0A961958260.

Wilson, Pam. "Welcoming Babies With Down Syndrome." Babycenter.com. Available online. URL: http://www.babycenter.com/refcap/baby/babydevelopment/1817.html.

Winders, Patricia C. "Why Physical Therapy?" Down Syndrome: Health Issues. Available online. URL: http://www.ds-health.com/physther.htm.

Zellweger, H. "Is Down's Syndrome A Modern Disease?" *The Lancet* 2 (1968): 458.

Zori, Roberto T., Desmond A. Schatz, Harry Ostrer, Charles A. Williams, Rebecca Spillar and William J. Riley. "Relationship of Autoimmunity to Thyroid Dysfunction in Children and Adults with Down Syndrome." American Journal of Medical Genetics Supplement 7 (1990): 238–241.

FURTHER READING

Bakely, Donald. *Down Syndrome, One Family's Journey: Beth Exceeds Expectations.* Cambridge, MA: Brookline Books, 2002.

Cohen, William I. (Ed.), Lynn Nadel, Myra E. Madnick. *Down Syndrome: Visions for the 21st Century.* New York: John Wiley & Sons, 2002.

Junot, Dan, Randy Orgeron, ed., and Jerry Franc, contributor. *Jackie, The Heart Warming, Inspirational True Story of a Remarkable Down Syndrome Girl: Plus, Parables for Parents of Down Syndrome Children.* Thibodaux, LA: Center For Special Services, 2002.

Kingsley, Jason, and Mitchell Levitz. *Count Us In: Growing Up with Down Syndrome.* New York: Harcourt Brace & Co., 1994.

Lambke, Brian, and Tom Lambke. *I Just Am: A Story of Down Syndrome Awareness and Tolerance.* Chandler, Arizona: Five Star Publications, Inc., 2006.

MacLeod, Kent. *Down Syndrome and Vitamin Therapy.* Canada: Kemanso Publishing, 2003.

McDaniel, Jo Beth. *A Special Kind of Hero: Chris Burke's Own Story.* New York: Doubleday, 1991.

Rivera, Geraldo. *Willowbrook: A Report on How It Is And Why It Doesn't Have To Be That Way.* New York: Random House, 1972.

Rogers, Dale Evans. *Angel Unaware, 50th Anniversary Edition.* Tarrytown, NY: Fleming H. Revell Company, 2004.

Rondal, Jean A. *The Adult with Down Syndrome: A New Challenge to Society*, New York: John Wiley & Sons, 2004.

WEB SITES

Famous People with Down Syndrome
http://www.about-down-syndrome.com/famous-people-with-down-syndrome.html

General Sensory Stimulation for Infants
http://www.csdsa.org/artthera.asp

Genetics Principles and Methods
http://groups.msn.com/BrainScience/geneticsprinciplesand methods.msnw

Hypothyroidism in Children with Down Syndrome
http://www.thyroid-info.com/articles/downsyndrome.htm

A New Day for Kids With Down's
http://www.naturalsolutionsmag.com/index.cfm/fuseaction/ articleSearch.article/articleID/8520

Trisomy 21: The Story of Down's Syndrome
http://www.ds-health.com/trisomy.htm

PICTURE CREDITS

INDEX

ABOUT THE AUTHOR

Dr. F. Fay Evans-Martin has a dual background in the areas of biopsychology and pharmacology. She earned a doctorate in psychology from the University of Georgia, a master's degree in pharmacology from the Medical College of Georgia, and a bachelor's degree in biology from Georgia Southern University. Her primary research interests are in neuroprotection and learning and memory. Research she has engaged in includes cholinergic research in short-term memory at the Medical College of Georgia, research in neuroprotection and learning and memory at the University of Georgia, spinal cord injury research at the University of Alabama at Birmingham, and nicotine self-administration research at the University of Pittsburgh. Evans-Martin has also taught undergraduate psychology courses, most recently at the University of Louisville. She is the mother of two sons, Shawn and Eric.

She dedicates her book:
With gratitude to Dr. Gary Heffner,
With love to Shawn and Eric, and
With honor to my loving Creator